Dear Barbara,

It was fun being with you!

Best to R. I.

Pat

Pasta for Men Only

Patricia Gambarelli

Patricia Gambarelli

Almar Books
Shallotte, NC
www.almarbooks.com

Pasta for Men Only by Patricia Gambarelli

Published by Almar Books
www.almarbooks.com

ISBN: 0-9740983-9-6

Book and Jacket Design by Bookmasters, Inc.
Original artwork by Suzanne Hunady

Applied for Library of Congress Cataloging-in-Publication Data.

First Edition
Printed in the United States of America

10 9 8 7 6 5 4 3 2

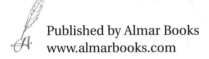

For my grandchildren:
Lexi, Kathleen, Ian, Trish, Peter, and Janna

Contents

Acknowledgments	ix
Introduction	xi

SECTION I
Getting Started

Pasta Primer	2
Do's and Don'ts for Perfect Pasta	3
Classic Italian Sauces and Cheeses	4
Extra Virgin Olive Oil	5
Balsamic Vinegar (Aceto Balsamicico)	6
Pantry Tips	7
List of Abbreviations	7

SECTION II
Sauces

Tomato—The Magical Fruit	10
Basic Tomato Sauce I	11
Basic Tomato Sauce II	12
Fresh Tomato and Basil Sauce	13
Sun-dried Tomato Sauce	14
Porcini Tomato Sauce	15
Meat Sauces—Bolognese Sauce: A Classic	16
Bolognese Tomato and Meat Sauce	17
Lasagne al Forno Made with No-Boil Noodles	18
Tomato Sauce with Sweet Sausage	20
Tomato Prosciutto Sauce	22
In No Time Flat—Dishes that Come Together in a Flash	23
Spaghetti Aglio e Olio (Garlic and Oil)	24
Spaghetti alla Puttanesca	25
Pasta with Butter and Parmesan Cheese	26
Egg Pappardelle with Mushroom Sauce	27

Some Like it Hot—Sauces with a Kick 28
Fra Diavolo Sauce with Linguine 29
Rigatoni all' Arrabbiata 30
Amatriciana Sauce with Bucatini 32
Bigoli with Anchovy Sauce 33
Capellini Capricoiosi (Spicy Capellini) 34
Say Cheese! 35
Pasta Penne with Tomato, Cream, and Five Cheeses 36
Penne and Zucchini with an Egg and Cheese Bonus 38
Fettuccine alla Carbonara 39
Pesto and Goat Cheese Sauce 40
Gorgonzola Sauce 41
Creamy Garlic Mushroom Sauce 42
Eat Your Veggies—Vegetable Sauces & Dishes 43
My Mother's Pesto Sauce, Amended 45
Pasta Primavera 46
Penne in an Artichoke Porcini Sauce 48
Angel Hair Pasta wrapped in Eggplant 50
Pan-Fried Zucchini Blossoms 52

SECTION III
The Sea's Bounty

Calamari in a Tomato Sauce 54
Rudy's White Clam Sauce for Linguine 56
Nina's Shrimp Scampi with Campanile 58
Johnny's Quick Mussel Sauce for Spaghetti 60
Penne with Seared Sea Scallops and Asparagus in a Basil Sauce 61
Vermicelli with Crab Meat in a Tomato-Cream Sauce 63
Spinach Fettuccini with Smoked Salmon 64
Lasagna di Mare 65

SECTION IV
Do-It-Yourself Dough

Fresh Pasta 68
Food Processor Dough (Ravioli) 70
Ravioli with a Duck and Spinach Filling in a Porcini-Cream Sauce 73
My Mother's Genoese Ravioli Filling 75

Crespelle—Pasta's Alter Ego 77
Cannelloni Filled with Three Cheeses 78
Gnocchi: Potato Dumplings 81
Potato Gnocchi 82
Gnocchi Verde 84
Ricotta Gnocchi in a Pink Vodka Sauce 86
Gnocchi alla Romana 88
Gnocchi with Butter and Sage 90
Time for a Spaghettata 91
Homemade Bread 93
Rudy's Tuscan Bread 94
Amaretto Mousse 96

SECTION V
Beyond Pasta

My Mother's Minestrone, Genoa Style 98
Caviar Eclipse 100
Pepperoni Batter Bread 101
Sausage Bread 102
Focaccia with Sage 104
Boned Chicken in a Wine Sauce 106
Veal Stew 107
Asparagus with Parmesan Cheese 109
Zucchini Soufflé 110
Sally Lunn—For the Morning After 111
Biscotti—A Dunking Cookie, Maybe 112
Biscotti di Prato 113
Anise Biscotti 114
Tiramisu 115
Panna Cotta 117
Biscuit Tortoni 118

Wine Terminology 119
The Partnership of Wine and Cheese 120
The Partnership of Wine and Food 121
Glossary of Culinary Terms 122
About the Author 124
About the Artist 124

Acknowledgments

Thanks to…

My friends in New York, the core group who brought so many aspiring cooks to the classes—Sandra Capri, Joan D'Addario, Lori Esposito, Lucy Ricotta, Joan Vizza, Gail Romanoff, and Angela Melchione. Thank you for taking an Italian Flyer with me. They came curious, and stayed, bringing many new friends. I did a lot of screaming for attention in my cramped kitchen in those days, but they never wavered, just cautioned, "be careful, she's mad today." They will be my friends to the end.

Giuliano Bugialli, for teaching me the intricacies of Italian cooking. He became a friend through the magic of pasta.

My college classmate, Fran Sidlo. We have been sisters under the skin for more years than I like to admit. She washed dishes, cleaned up after the classes, and ate the leftover pasta for breakfast as her only reward. Real friends do that sort of thing.

All the men in my classes who inspired this book. I am in awe of your self-effacing attitudes. No pretences, just the burning desire to want to be good cooks. Thank you for your unabashed trust in me.

I owe an enormous debt of gratitude to my Writer's Bloc friends. They let me in their elite group of aspiring authors, probably because they wondered who would ever be insane enough to think about writing a cookbook. But from day one they couldn't have been more supportive. I should say, relentless. Mark Smith, Don Glander, Jack DeGroot, Deloris Gausch, and Claire Connelly persisted, encouraged, edited, and tested recipes until I realized I had no way out. And to Brian McLaughlin, who, from day one, said it could be done.

My many friends in Sea Trail, and to my Gourmet Club members who constantly asked about the book until I could no longer hide; thank you for letting me joyfully say, "It's done."

My men friends at Sea Trail and beyond, who anxiously awaited an e-mail recipe attachment "to test." I am forever in your debt. You critiqued, sautéed, baked, puréed and very often, changed 10 minutes cooking time to 12. Your questions and suggestions were always taken under advisement. As a result, the recipes are more complete. This project led me to a new appreciation of the male mindset. My thanks to Don Glander, Jim Libby, Bill Taylor, Tom King, Ron McGurn, Lou Lisboa, John Lupi, Ralph Gardner, Stephen Saia, Rudy Ulrich, and my son-in-law, Paul Simmons, (the undisputed king of St. Louis barbecued ribs), for testing pasta recipes in the search for glitches.

What could have I done without Ellen Lehrer, my persistent grammarian, who assured me that I could fly in cyberspace and still survive? She encouraged me to chuck my typewriter and travel in the new world. Her keen eye for dangling participles brought me back to English 101.

Thanks to Mark Smith, my mentor. I give my heartfelt appreciation for his encouragement and enthusiasm in all things literary. Thankfully, there is no limit to his patience. Nikki Smith deserves an enormous amount of credit for tying up all the loose ends in the manuscript and accomplishing it so efficiently.

Thanks to all who looked for missing caps, stray commas, cups, teaspoons, or salt to taste omissions. Don Glander, the comma king, Sally Vuillet and eagle-eye Gloria Taylor, thank you for taking the time to carefully read the manuscript. I'm grateful to my daughter-in-law, Peggy, who used her legal expertise to trim the verbiage.

Sue King provided invaluable assistance. Nothing I could ever do to try her patience, worked! She was the stability, the calm, the sounding board and the friend that every cookbook writer needs in her computer kitchen.

There is another Sue in the pasta pot, my illustrator, Sue Hunady. Her whimsical drawings brought pasta shapes to life on these pages. She captured the focus of the book so completely and always with so much enthusiasm. She stacked up boxes of pasta and bottles of wine and vermouth in her studio and made the whole thing so much fun. I am forever in her debt.

Thanks to my family for making me stick with it. Bobby grabbed a yellow legal pad a couple of years ago and forced me to write a Table of Contents with him. I still have that scratch pad. It occupies a special place in my heart. Johnny and my daughter-in-law, Lynn, tempted me with so many gift cookbooks that I was bound to jump into the fray. According to John, everything about pasta is a slam dunk. To my daughter, Nina, who, from the time she was a little girl, cooked with me in my kitchen, and made everything look and taste better. Thank you for always listening and encouraging me from so many miles away. But, there are too many missing "Let's cook together," moments.

Thanks to my grandchildren, to whom this book is dedicated. I hope you will continue to cook, all the while remembering your roots and thinking of me when you do.

And finally, to my husband, Rudy, whose reputation as the King of Bread clearly overshadows anything I do in my kitchen. He doesn't understand my love/hate relationship with the computer, but he does know how much I love him.

Introduction

When I decided to open a cooking school in my home, the progression from my career in chemistry to cooking seemed to be a credible leap. The time had come to unite my passion for the food of my Italian heritage with my desire to teach. I firmly believed I could remember and reproduce dishes from my mother's recipes that were safely stored in the back of my mind. The concept seemed simple enough; create a dish, taste, and then type. Little did I realize the daunting task that lay ahead. It became apparent, rather quickly, that a good recipe doesn't magically appear. Accurate measurements, a proper combination of quality ingredients, cooking times, and portion size were just a few of the controls. Was it possible to really write a recipe that took every foreseeable misstep out of the mix? Faced with requirements that seemed too formidable to conquer on my own, I made the trek to Manhattan to take cooking classes with Giuliano Bugialli and Marcella Hazan, the masters of Italian cooking. They awakened in me the desire to further explore my Italian heritage and its incomparable cuisine.

I called on some women friends to be willing students for private cooking lessons. It was then that I embarked on the voyage that was to immeasurably enrich my life. Word quickly spread on Long Island about my private Italian cooking classes. Soon, twelve aspiring cooks were working in my cramped kitchen twice a week. Each class concluded at the dining room table where we tasted and critiqued the recipes and appropriate wines, which my husband Rudy, selected. Guest chefs and dessert and bread-making workshops quickly filled the calendar.

Not to be outdone by their wives, a group of men asked to learn some of the same cooking techniques. Before long, bachelors living on their own, young executives, single family members, and men from all walks of life and professions attended the classes. The men became accomplished pasta makers, accumulating recipes for ravioli, cannelloni, lasagne, and a treasure-trove of sauces. Obviously, the role of men in the kitchen had changed dramatically over the years. Men were eager to improve their cooking skills, were tired of take-out, and wanted an alternative to the barbecue grill.

The thrust of the Pasta for Men Only classes was twofold: expand the cook's culinary repertoire and move into the twenty-first century with dishes that could be prepared ahead. I formulated recipes that easily adapted to their lifestyles. Many were "do-ahead recipes" that could be made in stages or frozen. It enabled them to pop a previously-prepared dish in the oven for dinner. Their ability to make filled pastas with fresh dough took their cooking skills to the top of the chart. In addition to everyday meals, they wanted recipes and a game plan for hosting dinner parties. Subsequently, Pasta and Beyond emerged. In those classes we delved into recipes for meat, poultry, fish, pizzas, breads, and desserts. These popular classes lasted for eleven years. Then, when I received an offer to write a Food and Wine column for a Long Island newspaper I jumped at the chance. It meant reviewing and dining in some of the most prestigious restaurants in the Big Apple.

This love for everything culinary must be genetic. At the turn of the century my maternal grandfather Tony, an Italian immigrant from Genoa, opened a groceria in Greenwich Village. He imported prosciutto and Parmigiano Reggiano and other fine products from Italy and stocked wines from California. My father owned and operated a wholesale French bakery in New York City for over forty years with my paternal grandfather. They supplied their incomparable baguettes, whole-wheat Vienna loaves, and White Mountain rolls to retail shops the length and breadth of Manhattan Island.

As a youngster, I learned to be an experienced food shopper. My mother often entrusted me with the task of buying fruit and vegetables from pushcarts on Bleecker Street in Greenwich Village and to select meat and poultry from Mr. Dorato's butcher shop on MacDougal Street. It was not unusual for mother to send me to Raffetto's on West Houston Street to buy two pounds of freshly-made sheets of pasta so she could prepare her Genoese version of ravioli for that night's dinner.

Undoubtedly, my stint in chemistry labs improved my organizational skills, made me take notice of quantities, and best of all gave me the confidence to experiment. When I married Rudy, whose entire career was spent in the wine industry, I came full circle. Is it any wonder that our children are all tuned in to good food and great wines?

In my classes, zealous cooks were turning out great dishes from traditional recipes. But, best of all, friendships were forged that enriched each of our lives in so many ways. We went to some of New York's finest restaurants, enjoyed parties on Long Island's North Shore, celebrated New Year's Eve at Windows on the World in the Twin Towers, traveled to Italy, France, Germany and Spain, and even soared over the Verazzano Bridge in a single engine plane.

I hope this book will take you on a pleasurable journey and to a place where good food and friendship meet.

Section I

Getting Started

This section will get you started down the road to some wonderful Italian dishes. In it, you will find a very short history lesson to put you in the mood, some basic terminology to give you confidence, a list of essential ingredients to keep in your kitchen, and some quick tips—all designed to help you cook like a pro.

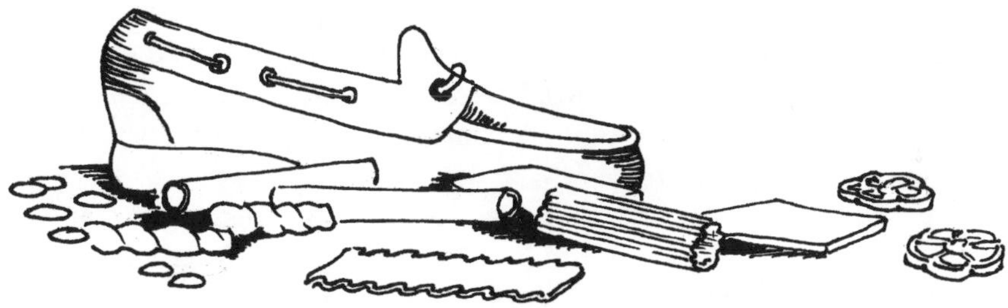

PASTA PRIMER

When I started to write this book, I knew it would take me in many directions, but I wasn't prepared for the wealth of information I found in my research. Let's begin at the beginning. The word "pasta" comes from the Italian phrase *paste alimentari: paste* meaning dough made from flour and water and *alimentari* denoting nourishment. Most history books credit Marco Polo with pasta's arrival from the Orient but records show that the Chinese were eating noodles as far back as 1700 B.C. In America, Thomas Jefferson became a promoter of pasta after falling in love with it on a trip to Europe. Result: A pasta-making machine was shipped to Virginia in 1789. Perhaps Mr. Jefferson is responsible for pasta going "mainstream" and into the diets of millions of Americans.

Because it appears on your table and in restaurants so often, it seems appropriate to understand the variety of forms of pasta: the filled and the flat, the tubes and the twists, the ribbons and the curves, the reeds and the muffs, the stars and the letters, and the long and the short of it. If you think about it, some combinations are obvious. Tube pastas like penne and rigatoni draw the sauce inside, as do ziti and perciatelli—these shapes are generally classified as macaroni. Shell shapes gather both the sauce and pieces of vegetable or meat. Texture is a very important consideration, too. Delicate pastas or string pastas fare well when matched with delicate sauces. Robust sauces go with the sturdier pastas. The thinner, dry pastas: capelli d'angelo (angel hair), capellini, fidelini, spaghettini, and vermicelli are not overwhelmed by subtle sauces such as seafood, vegetables, butter, and cheese.

The National Pasta Foundation estimates that there are 150 different shapes made in this country.

If we consider all the available dies and varying lengths, we could conceivably add hundreds to that number. So esteemed is pasta in Italy that the Chamber of Commerce in Bologna, Italy's gastronomic capital, enshrined a solid gold tagliatelle indicating its ideal thickness and weight in a sealed glass case. Pasta's unique versatility and nutritional value has contributed to its mass appeal. It suits every course on the menu, from appetizers to entrees and desserts, and complements a wide variety of foods—cheese, vegetables, meats, fish, poultry, shellfish, and eggs.

Nutritionally, pasta is in perfect accord with the Food Pyramid. It is low in calories and provides valuable amounts of complex carbohydrates, protein, B vitamins, and iron. Of course, the accompanying sauces determine the calorie count of a pasta dish, but pasta itself is low in calories. A two-ounce portion of spaghetti has 200 calories and yields forty grams of carbohydrate, seven grams of protein, one gram of fat, and no cholesterol.

Pasta is made from durum wheat, a high protein, hard wheat selected for its flavor, color, and texture. Pasta made from durum wheat is the easiest to digest, has a low starch content, and is high in protein. Nutrition-conscious Americans have now come to realize that rich sauces, not the pasta itself, are the dieter's downfall. Fettuccine Alfredo has been labeled a "heart attack on a plate" and justifiably so. But further studies indicate that most pasta dishes are heart healthy. Portion size! Portion size! Portion size! Think 1/4 pound per person as the Italians do.

The Do's and Don'ts for Perfect Pasta

1. Don't overcook pasta. Perfectly cooked pasta is cooked to *al dente,* firm to the bite. Taste it.
2. Don't skimp on the water. Use 6–8 quarts of water for each pound of fresh or dry pasta.
3. Add salt to the water after it comes to a boil. Adding salt at the outset gives the pasta a metallic taste.
4. Don't break the pasta before cooking unless it's unusually long.
5. Don't add oil to the water. The sauce will slip and slide off the pasta.
6. Don't rinse pasta. The starch on the surface helps the noodle to combine with the sauce.
7. Don't over-drain pasta. If it's too dry, it's difficult to blend in the sauce. Give the colander a couple of shakes and turn it into a warm bowl or into the pan containing the sauce.
8. Don't over-sauce pasta. There should be no extra sauce over it or at the bottom of the bowl.
9. Do reheat pasta in the microwave. Only the water molecules are heated. The pasta will be warm but not dried out.
10. Do enjoy a bowl of perfectly prepared pasta.

Classic Italian Sauces

Accuighe—anchovies with garlic, oil, and parsley

Aglio e Olio—garlic and olive oil

Alfredo—butter, cream, and freshly-grated Parmigiano

Amatriciana —tomatoes, chopped bacon, onion, red pepper, and Romano cheese

Bolognese—meat sauce with tomatoes, wine, vegetables, milk, and nutmeg

Burro—butter and Parmesan cheese

Carbonara—sautéed prosciutto or bacon with eggs

Frutti di mare—seafood sauce

Pesto—oil, grated cheese, pine nuts, basil, and garlic that has been pounded into a paste

Primavera—vegetables, butter, and Parmesan cheese

Garlic, parsley, and basil are basic ingredients in Italian pasta recipes. Herbs are limitless: fennel, marjoram, mint, oregano, rosemary, sage, and thyme. Black pepper, white pepper, cayenne, and chilies are red-hot choices right now.

Cheese

There are also many classic Italian cheeses. Besides the ever-popular Parmigiano-Reggiano, Pecorino Romano, Mozzarella, and Ricotta, many other varieties are easily interchanged in a recipe.

Asiago—the "poor man's Parmesan." A hard cow's milk cheese good for grating.

Chevre—a mild goat's milk cheese, creamy when melted.

Gorgonzola—s creamy blue-veined cheese, made from cow's milk. Excellent for sauce.

Gruyére—a firm, nutty cheese made from cow's milk.

Ricotta—a soft, mild cheese made from whey or whole cow's milk and used in filled pastas.

Parmesan—a hard, tangy cheese made from cow's milk and aged two years. Parmigiano-Reggiano, often referred to as the *King of Cheeses* comes from an area near Parma, Italy. The words *Parmigiano-Reggiano*

are imprinted all over the rind. *Grana padano is a less expensive cheese and is not a substitute for the real thing.*

Romano—Italy's oldest cheese, a hard grating cheese made from sheep's milk. Also called Pecorino, Romano is sharper and zestier than Parmesan.

Fontina—a soft cheese made in Piedmont.

Mascarpone—a fresh Italian cream cheese with a short shelf life. It is the main component in Tiramisu.

Mozzarella—a soft cheese made in America from cow's milk. Authentic mozzarella is always salted. The plastic-covered mozzarella from the supermarket cannot compare to fresh mozzarella.

Extra-virgin olive oil

The craze for Italian food in America has produced an influx of products from Europe—not all of them up to snuff. A case in point: extra-virgin olive oil. It's not an exaggeration to say that a good rule of thumb when buying extra-virgin oil is "it never tastes better than the day it was made." Responsible producers of top-notch oil include a harvest date on the label and, sometimes, include a date by which the oil should be consumed. Do not buy oil past the consumption date or more than a year and a half past the harvest date. Specialty gourmet shops, generally speaking, offer top-quality oils from all over the world. Many supermarkets, too, stock quality brand names.

The name Extra-Virgin is the designation for premium quality oil made from the first cold press (containing a maximum of 1% oleic acid). The olives are pressed and processed without heat or solvents. The color varies from gold to deep green.

Virgin Olive Oil is also made from the first cold press, but contains from 1 to 3.3 % oleic acid.

Olive oil has an acidity level higher than 3.3%, but is treated with solvents to remove the excess acidity. The refining process, however, has no effect on the nutrients in the olive oil.

Light olive oil is an American marketing title. This oil is refined with little flavor and color. With 120 calories per tablespoon, the calorie count is equivalent to that of olive oil.

Leaving a bottle open for just a month dramatically reduces the oil's quality. It should be stored, tightly-sealed, in a cool dark place, and never kept near the stove. Refrigerating the oil is an absolute no-no, as the moisture formed from refrigeration will make the oil rancid.

The best extra-virgin oils are produced in three regions in Europe: Italy, Spain, and Greece. Experts agree that the best oil comes from Tuscany because this area in Italy is one of the coldest olive-growing regions in the world. The majority of olives are green when harvested, creating a fruity-flavored, peppery oil. Spain produces more olive oil than any other country worldwide. There are many good oils from Spain, but very few emerge as exceptional. Greece produces, dollar for dollar, some of the best oils. Seventy-five percent of the Greek production is extra-virgin. They come highly recommended, especially from the Kalamata region, which produces the Kalamata olive.

Balsamic vinegar *(aceto balsamicico)*

On our first trip to Italy, we were enjoying a delightful lunch when I persuaded the owner of the restaurant to give me a bottle of her Balsamic vinegar to take back to the States. I trudged my treasure from north to south for three weeks. Each sprinkling of the delightful vinegar in the years that followed our return home brought back memories of magnificent food and gracious people.

Modena, the hometown of Luciano Pavarotti and Ferrari cars, is also famous for the production of balsamic vinegar, a vinegar which cannot be successfully produced anywhere else in the world. The Modenese were making and using it as early as 1046. Many families have a "batteria" (a set of vinegar barrels) in their attics and consider balsamico to be a prized family possession. So precious is it, that it was often included in the bride-to-be's dowry.

The climate, the low-lying landscape, the white Trebbiano grapes, and the different-sized casks of chestnut, oak, juniper, cherry, and mulberry woods are the prerequisites for the production of aceto balsamico. The Trebbiano grapes are harvested and pressed and must be immediately drained from the skins and seeds. The juice is boiled in a long cooking process until the grapes' sugar is caramelized. It is then filtered, cooled, placed in a wooden barrel, and then racked through different types of wooden kegs. Unlike wine vinegar, which converts alcohol to acid, balsamic vinegar is produced by converting sugar to acid.

This painstaking process continues for a minimum of ten years. The result is a remarkably aromatic liquid rich in flavor, sweet and sour at the same time. The vinegar enhances pastas, risotti, grilled or roasted meats and poultry, fritters and fritattas, fruits, and vegetables.

The balsamico should be added at the end of the cooking time so as not to diminish its distinctive quality.

Pantry Tips

Must Have

Stainless steel pots	12-inch Chef's knife	Can opener
12-inch skillet	Slotted spoon	Cheese grater
8-inch non-stick skillet	Long handled fork	Cutting boards
8 qt. Pasta pot	Whisk	Mixing bowls
Sauté pan	Rolling pin	Olive oil
9x13x3-inch ovenproof pan	Spatula	Peppermill
	Vegetable peeler	Measuring cups
6-inch Paring knife	Colander	Measuring spoons

Should Have

Pasta machine	Potato ricer	Food mill
Food processor	Ravioli cutter	Heavy duty mixer
Blender	Pastry scraper	Rolling pin
Crêpe pan	Sieve	

Would Be Nice

Cleaver	Extra virgin olive oil	Chef's pan
Serrated bread knife	Zester/grater	12x17-inch baking sheet
Good quality Balsamic vinegar	Clam knife	
	Springform pan	

List of Abbreviations

c. = Cup(s)	oz. = Ounce(s)	qt(s). = Quart(s)
g. = Grams(s)	pkg. = Package	Tbsp(s). = Tablespoon(s)
lb(s). = Pound(s)	pt(s). = Pint(s)	Tsp(s). = Teaspoon(s)

Section II

Sauces

I think there was a time in America when Italian cooking neglected the art of presentation. Chefs were content to focus instead, on regional cooking and quality ingredients. But, the explosion of information on world-wide cuisines, on television and the Internet, emboldened innovative American chefs to broaden their horizons. Sticking to their quality-first credo, they have nuanced their recipes, resulting in new and tasteful dishes. Inspired by their new-found creativity, their dishes are attractively presented but not in a pretentious way.

TOMATO—THE MAGICAL FRUIT

Webster defines magic as a "supernatural art or agency that works with a wonderful effect." There is no denying that this luscious fruit weaves a magical spell in mid-summer and early fall when the tomato takes us on so many culinary excursions.

Tomato recipes abound: Bread Soup with Tomatoes, Tomato Salads, Filled Tomatoes, Baked and Stuffed Tomatoes, Stewed Tomatoes, Soufflés, Pizzas, Salsas, Fried Green Tomatoes, and a myriad of sauces that accompany seafood, fish, poultry, meats, and pastas. How versatile can you get?

The tomato is a nutritional gem. A 5- to 8-ounce tomato has about 27 calories, 1.4 grams protein, 6 grams carbohydrate, 0.2 grams fat, 0.6 grams fiber, 1000 IU vitamin A, 28 IU vitamin C and calcium, sodium, phosphorous, and potassium.

The tomato began its journey as a wild plant in South America in what are now the countries of Peru, Ecuador, and Bolivia. After its domestication in pre-Columbian times it was sold in Mexico City by vendors who blended it with Aji (hot red pepper), pepitas (pumpkin seeds), and chile verdes (hot green peppers) to make a highly savory juice.

The tomato appeared in Spain in the early sixteenth century where it was valued for its magical and medicinal properties. It reached Italy in the seventeenth century when it began to appear and be accepted as an edible food. Although the Spanish brought it into the country, it apparently took more than a century and the ingenuity of the Italians of southern Italy to bring the tomato and pasta together. Only in the late eighteenth and early nineteenth centuries did gourmets and leading chefs "officially" endorse the tomato, and it was only in the nineteenth century that it became a common food.

In 1835, William Underwood, an American, opened a factory in Boston and developed an industrial process to can tomatoes to save us from the fresh tomato-less winter doldrums.

The tomato is still on its journey, touching us all in some form or other, waiting patiently to be "discovered" in another recipe.

Basic Tomato Sauce I

(Enough for 1 pound of pasta)

Wine Suggestion: Chianti

I had a group of young architects in my Pasta for Men Only *classes in New York. They declared it to be their favorite sauce recipe because "it's fast, easy, freezable, and it freed them from the deli." It's a versatile sauce. Adding shrimp or scallops gives this tomato sauce a seafood spin.*

Dry vermouth contains about eleven herbs and aromatics, so why not opt for vermouth instead of dry white wine? It may be in the cupboard poised for martini-making.

When the spirit moves you, double or triple this recipe, then ladle the sauce into varying sizes of plastic containers or baggies and freeze. Thawed, it will be a jump start for other dishes in your repertoire.

Don't settle for just any brand or type of canned tomato. Use whole or diced plum tomatoes from Italy or California.

1/4 c. olive oil
1 small onion, minced, about 1/2 c.
1 garlic clove, minced
1/4 c. dry white wine or dry vermouth
1 28-oz. can Italian plum tomatoes with their juice
1 Tbsp. slivered fresh basil leaves or 1 tsp. dried
salt and freshly ground pepper to taste

1. In a 2 qt. saucepan, heat the olive oil until it glazes over.
2. Add the onions and cook over moderate heat until they soften but are not browned, about 8 minutes. Add the garlic and sauté 2 minutes.
3. Add the white wine or vermouth, and bring to a boil to dissipate the alcohol.
4. Add the tomatoes, basil, and salt and pepper. Set the heat to low, and simmer with the pot partially covered for about 40 minutes. Stir occasionally.
5. Pass the sauce through a food mill into a bowl. The sauce will be slightly thick and smooth.

Basic Tomato Sauce II

(Enough for 1 pound of pasta)

The vegetables in this recipe produce a thick sauce. Pass the finished sauce through a food mill or process in a food processor if desired.

WINE SUGGESTION: Valpolicella

1/4 c. olive oil
1 medium onion, minced
1 carrot, minced
1 stalk celery, minced
(You could also combine the onion, carrot, and celery in a food processor and pulse a few times.)
1/4 c. dry white wine or dry vermouth
1 28 oz. can whole plum tomatoes, coarsely chopped
2 Tbsp. minced Italian flat-leaf parsley
pinch oregano (optional)
salt and freshly ground pepper to taste

1. In a medium saucepan, heat oil over medium heat.
2. Add onion, carrot, and celery and cook until the vegetables are softened, about 10–12 minutes.
3. Add wine or vermouth. Turn up the heat for a few minutes to burn off the alcohol.
4. Add the tomatoes and parsley.
5. Add oregano, salt, and pepper. Simmer, slightly covered, for about 30 minutes.
6. Process if desired.

Fresh Tomato and Basil Sauce

(Serves 4–6)

Don't pass up the opportunity to taste the glories of the summer. Tomatoes and fresh herbs are basic to this simple sauce.

WINE SUGGESTION: Bardolino

1 lb. Farfalle (butterfly-shaped pasta)
About a dozen ripe plum tomatoes, peeled, seeded, and coarsely chopped
1 clove garlic, minced
4 Tbsp. extra-virgin olive oil
6–8 fresh sweet basil leaves, cut in thin slices
salt and freshly ground pepper to taste

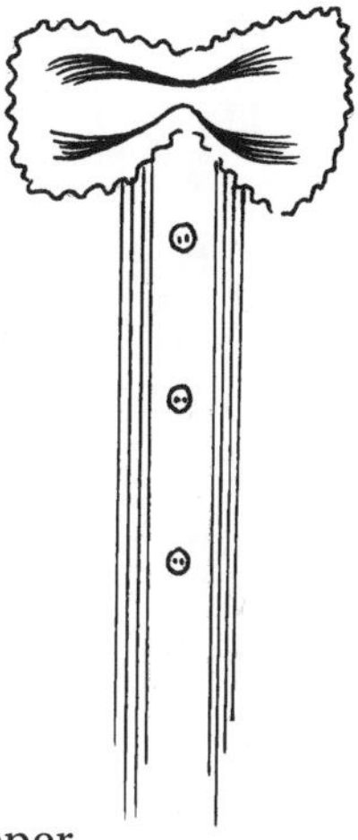

1. Remove the stem end of tomato and score the opposite end with a shallow "x" shape. Immerse the tomatoes in boiling water for 30 seconds. Plunge them in ice water and, using a knife or your fingers, peel off the skin.
2. Cut the tomatoes in half crosswise. Gently squeeze out the seeds and coarsely chop.
3. In a medium skillet, heat the oil over moderate heat, add the garlic, and sauté the garlic until golden. Do not burn the garlic!
4. Add the tomatoes and basil. Season with salt and pepper and simmer, stirring occasionally, for 10 minutes.
5. While the sauce is cooking, cook the pasta in boiling, salted water until *al dente*. Drain the pasta into a large bowl and toss with the sauce.
6. Garnish with additional basil leaves. Serve with freshly grated Parmesan or Romano cheese.

Sun-Dried Tomato Sauce

(Serves 4)

Good quality sun-dried tomatoes, packed in oil, are available in grocery stores and supermarkets.

WINE SUGGESTION: Zinfandel

3/4 lb. Campanelle
3 Tbsp. olive oil
1 Tbsp. unsalted butter
2 shallots, thinly sliced
2 garlic cloves, minced
2/3 c. chicken broth, low salt
1/2 c. heavy cream
1 8-oz. can tomato sauce
1/2 c. sun-dried tomatoes, packed in oil, drained and coarsely chopped
10 Kalamata olives, pitted and coarsely chopped
freshly ground pepper, to taste
2 Tbsp. Italian flat-leaf parsley, minced
4 Tbsp. Parmesan cheese, freshly grated

1. In a large sauté or chef's pan, warm the oil and butter over moderately low heat.
2. Add the shallots and cook 2 minutes.
3. Add the garlic and cook 1–2 minutes.
4. Add the chicken broth and simmer 3 minutes.
5. Whisk in the cream, tomato sauce, and sun-dried tomatoes. Stir until well blended. Cook over moderate heat, 8–10 minutes.
6. Stir in the olives, pepper, parsley, and Parmesan cheese.
7. Meanwhile, bring a large pot of water to a boil. Add salt. Cook the pasta to *al dente.* Drain and add the pasta to the skillet containing the sauce.
8. Serve in individual bowls and pass additional Parmesan cheese.

Porcini Tomato Sauce

(Serves 4–6)

Dry porcini mushrooms should be a staple in your pantry. Fresh porcini mushrooms fly in on a plane and are almost never available in the USA. Dried porcini are the next best option. Buy three or four ounces, store them in the freezer, and reconstitute with hot water when ready to use. They are relatively expensive but their intense flavor outweighs the cost. Porcini are available in Italian specialty shops and in most supermarkets.

WINE SUGGESTION: Merlot

1/4 c. olive oil
1 medium onion, minced
1 clove garlic, chopped fine
1 stalk celery, chopped fine
1 small carrot, chopped fine
2 Tbsp. minced Italian flat-leaf parsley
1/4 c. total dry and sweet vermouth in equal amounts
3/4 oz. dry porcini mushrooms, soaked in 1 cup hot water for 15 minutes. Drain and reserve the liquid. If necessary, decant the liquid through a paper filter to remove any residue. Set aside.
1 28-oz. can whole plum tomatoes, coarsely chopped.

1. Heat the oil in a saucepan over medium heat. Add the onions, garlic, celery, and carrot. Sauté until the vegetables are soft and translucent, about 10 minutes.
2. Add the parsley and vermouths. Cook 2 minutes to dispel the alcohol.
3. Add half the mushroom liquor to the saucepan.
4. Coarsely chop the porcini and add them along with the tomatoes, salt, and freshly ground pepper.
5. Simmer gently, uncovered, for 20–25 minutes.
6. Process the cooled sauce in a food processor if you prefer a smoother sauce.
7. Serve with your favorite pasta. Sprinkle generously with freshly grated Parmesan cheese.

Meat Sauces—Bolognese Sauce: A Classic

The classic recipe for Bolognese Sauce is logged at the Chamber of Commerce in Bologna. It is one of the few recipes in Italy that is officially codified. Traditionally, it is served with tagliatelle, tortellini, or lasagne verde.

There seem to be as many versions of Bolognese sauce as there are regions in Italy, each area using different combinations of ingredients. The standard recipe for the sauce starts with a *soffritto,* a combination of butter, onion, carrot, and celery sautéed in melted butter. The *soffritto* is then sautéed with beef, pork, veal, or prosciutto or a combination of all the meats. Good quality tomatoes are essential to the recipe. The Bolognese typically add milk or cream to impart a sweetness to the sauce. It is essential to cook the sauce at a bare simmer for two hours to blend the flavors.

The choice of ingredients depends on the cook and the availability of ingredients in each unique region of the country. Often, lean chopped beef, chicken livers, and tomato paste replace the usual ingredients. Notice the use of butter as opposed to olive oil in the preparation of the *soffritto.* Bologna's geographical proximity to France determines that city's predilection for butter.

According to Waverly Root, a Bolognese legend propounds that a nobleman's cook was so entranced with the color of Lucrezia Borgia's hair at a dinner party that he created tagliatelle—the fettuccine-like pasta often served with Bolognese sauce—to mimic her light flaxen hair.

Christmas dinner in Bologna traditionally begins with tortellini—small rings of pasta stuffed with pork, turkey, prosciutto, sausage, or cheese—served with Bolognese sauce. According to an anonymous article printed in 1874 in the *Bolognese Gazette,* "Tortellini is more essential than sun and a Saturday and love for a woman." In 1925, Ostilio Lucarini authored a play, *The Inventor of Tortellini.* It is the story of a cook who claimed to see his employer's wife sleeping in the nude. He fell in love with her and created, cooked, and served pasta made in the shape of her navel.

Bolognese Tomato and Meat Sauce

(Yield: 4 cups, enough for 1 pound of pasta or for Lasagne and Tortellini)

WINE SUGGESTION: Zinfandel

5 Tbsp. unsalted butter
1 medium sweet onion, finely chopped
1 carrot, skin scraped and finely chopped
1 celery stalk, finely chopped
1 lb. good quality lean beef, ground
1 c. dry white wine
1/2 c. whole milk
1/8 tsp. nutmeg
1/2 tsp. salt
freshly ground pepper to taste
1-28 oz. can whole plum tomatoes, seeded and coarsely chopped, with their juice

1. In a large heavy pot, melt the butter. A food processor does a good job of chopping the onion, carrot, and celery to create the *soffritto.* Add the *soffritto* to the pot and sauté over medium-low heat until the vegetables are soft but not browned, about 10 minutes.
2. Stir in the meat, making sure to break it up. Sauté, with stirring, until the meat loses its red color and is light pink.
3. Add the salt, pepper, and the wine and simmer gently until the alcohol dissipates, about 5 minutes.
4. Stir in the milk and stir to coat the meat. Add the nutmeg. Cook about 10 minutes.
5. Add the tomatoes. Cook the sauce, uncovered, at a bare simmer over very low heat for about 2 hours. Stir occasionally. Taste and correct for seasonings.

The sauce can be refrigerated for three days, covered, or frozen up to one month.

Lasagne al Forno—Made with no-boil noodles

(Serves 6–8)

Bolognese sauce can be made ahead, stored in the refrigerator up to three days or frozen. Balsamella and the cheese mixture can be made and held for a few hours before assembling the finished dish. Barilla pasta noodles are flat and resemble fresh lasagna sheets except they are dried and do not need to be boiled. There are other brands of no-boil lasagna on the market, but I consider Barilla to be a superior product.

WINE SUGGESTION: Cabernet Sauvignon or Chardonnay

Preheat oven to 375 degrees.

1 8-oz pkg. of no-boil lasagna (16 sheets)
1 recipe Bolognese sauce

Balsamella (Béchamel):

6 Tbsp. unsalted butter
1/2 c. all purpose flour
3 c. whole milk
salt to taste
1/8 tsp. freshly ground nutmeg, or to taste

1. In a medium saucepan, melt the butter.
2. Stir in the flour and cook over low heat, with stirring, until it colors, about 5 minutes.

3. Meanwhile, bring the milk to a boil.
4. Add the milk to the flour-butter mixture all at once. Stir with a wooden spoon or wire whisk until it thickens, about 5 minutes.
5. Stir in the salt and nutmeg.
6. Put a piece of wax paper directly on the sauce to keep a skin from forming. Set aside.

Cheese Mixture:

8 oz. whole milk mozzarella, coarsely grated
1 1/2 cups Parmesan cheese, freshly grated, reserve 1/4 cup

Mix the cheeses together, cover and set aside.

Assembly:

1. Butter a 9x13x3-inch oven-ready pan.
2. Spoon about 3/4 cup Bolognese sauce over the bottom of the pan.
3. Layer 4 sheets of lasagne, overlapping slightly. Spread about 3/4 cup sauce over all.
4. Spread 1/4 balsamella over the sauce.
5. Sprinkle with 1/4 cheese mixture.
6. Repeat steps 3, 4, and 5 three more times.
7. Bake for 55–60 minutes

Allow the lasagne to rest 15 minutes before serving.

The lasagne can be prepared up to 24 hours before serving. Cover and refrigerate. When ready to bake, allow 10–20 minutes more cooking time.

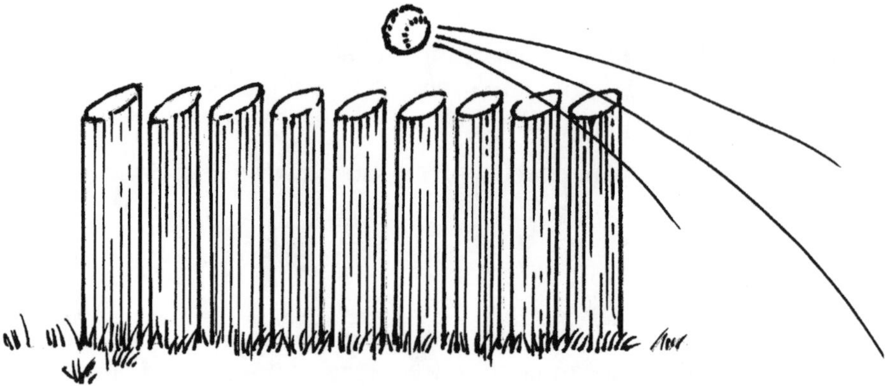

Tomato Sauce with Sweet Sausage

(Serves 4–6)

I always look for sweet sausage that doesn't contain fennel. For my taste, fennel overpowers the other flavors in a recipe. You can't always trust the labeling, however, because fennel may be hiding in the list of ingredients as "spices." But sweet or hot, fennel or not, it's your choice. Serve this one-dish dinner with a salad of mixed greens.

WINE SUGGESTION: Zinfandel

1 lb. Rigatoni
1 lb. ground Italian sweet sausage
2 Tbsp. olive oil
1 28-oz. can Italian plum tomatoes, puréed in a food mill
1 tsp. salt
1 tsp. dried oregano
freshly grated pepper
2 Tbsp. unsalted butter, softened
3/4 c. Parmesan cheese

1. In a large saucepan equipped with a cover, heat the oil.
2. Brown the sausage.
3. Add the puréed tomatoes and salt.

4. Cover and cook over moderately-low heat for about 45 minutes.
5. Add the oregano and pepper.
6. Simmer gently, uncovered, for 5–10 minutes, with stirring.
7. Meanwhile, cook the rigatoni in a large pot of boiling water until *al dente.*
8. Drain and toss the pasta with the softened butter and cheese. Stir in as much sauce as necessary to coat the pasta.
9. Portion the pasta into individual bowls. Add additional sauce if desired.

Tomato Prosciutto Sauce

(Enough for 1 pound of pasta)

WINE SUGGESTION: Verdicchio

2 Tbsp. olive oil
1 Tbsp. unsalted butter
4 oz. prosciutto, finely diced
1 small onion, minced
1 stalk celery, chopped fine
1 clove garlic, peeled and chopped fine
3 Tbsp. sweet vermouth
1 28 oz. can Italian plum tomatoes, coarsely chopped. Reserve the juice.
Salt and freshly ground pepper to taste
1 tsp. crumbled dry basil

1. In a large sauté pan, heat the oil over medium heat until it glazes over. Add the butter.
2. Add the diced prosciutto and cook, stirring constantly, until it is soft but not browned, about 2 minutes.
3. Reduce the heat to low, add the minced onion and celery. Cook, stirring constantly, until the vegetables are soft, about 5 minutes.
4. Add the garlic and cook for about 1 minute.
5. Add the vermouth, cook until the alcohol dissipates, about 2 minutes.
6. Add the tomatoes and their juice, salt and pepper, and the basil.
7. Simmer, partially covered, over medium heat, until the sauce thickens, about 25 minutes.

In No Time Flat—Dishes that Come Together in a Flash

The title says it all. Assemble the ingredients and start the sauce when the pasta goes into the pot. A simple salad on the side rounds out the light supper.

Spaghetti Aglio e Olio (garlic and oil)

(Serves 4–6)

Get rid of those hunger pangs when you arrive home after a night on the town. Whip up this dish in no time flat, but remember the Golden Rule: Never Serve Cheese with this recipe.

WINE SUGGESTION: Barbera

- 1 lb. Spaghetti
- 3 cloves garlic, minced by hand
- 1/2 c. extra-virgin olive oil
- salt and freshly ground pepper
- red pepper flakes
- 2 Tbsp. minced Italian flat-leaf parsley

1. Bring an ample amount of water to a rolling boil. Salt. Cook the pasta to *al dente.*
2. Meanwhile, add the oil to a small saucepan and sauté the garlic, over medium heat, for about 3 minutes. Do not let it brown.
3. When the pasta is cooked, drain into a bowl and toss with the sauce.
4. Season with salt and pepper and red pepper flakes, if desired
5. Stir in the parsley and serve immediately in individual bowls.

Spaghetti alla Puttanesca

a.k.a. "Harlot, Whore or Meretrice's Spaghetti"

(Serves 4–6)

As the story goes, in the 1950s, the brothels in Italy were owned by the state. The law allowed the ladies of the evening to shop for food only one day a week. Available fresh ingredients, therefore, were usually in short supply. Of necessity, their dishes became a creative affair, made from whatever was handy in the cupboard.
This recipe can be prepared quickly if you're on the run.

WINE SUGGESTION:
Barbaresco

- 1/4 c. olive oil
- 2 garlic cloves, minced
- 6 anchovy fillets, cut in pieces
- 1 28 oz. can whole tomatoes passed through a food mill, or diced tomatoes with their juice
- 8 pimento olives, sliced
- 8 pitted black olives, sliced
- 2 tsp. capers
- 1 tsp. dried basil
- 1/2 tsp. dried red pepper flakes
- freshly ground pepper to taste

1. In a sauté pan, add the oil and garlic and cook over low/medium heat.
2. Add the anchovies and cook until they start melting.
3. Add the tomatoes and simmer for about 10 minutes.
4. Add the olives, capers, basil, and pepper. Simmer uncovered for about 20 minutes, or until the sauce has thickened.

Serve on Spaghetti or another variety. It's your call.

Pasta with Butter and Parmesan Cheese

(Serves 4–6)

This is the simplest of all sauces and can accompany any favorite pasta, such as fettuccine, angel hair, or thin spaghetti. The sweet cream butter is also a perfect visual foil for green tagliatelle.

WINE SUGGESTION: Pinot Grigio

8 oz. pasta of choice
1/4 lb. unsalted butter (1 stick), melted
6 Tbsp. Parmesan cheese, freshly grated

1. Bring 6 qts. of water to a boil.
2. Add 1/2 tsp. salt.
3. Cook the pasta to *al dente.*
4. Pour the melted butter into a serving dish.
5. Drain the pasta and pour it into the serving dish.
6. Turn the pasta to evenly coat the strands, sprinkling cheese and tossing until everything is evenly coated.
7. Serve immediately on hot plates.

Egg Pappardelle with Mushroom Sauce

(Serves 6)

The flavors of fresh sliced mushrooms and minced fresh parsley, combined with butter and Parmesan cheese make for a delectable and elegant presentation. Imported dried pappardelle are readily available in most markets.

WINE SUGGESTION: Chablis

1 lb. imported Italian egg noodles
3/4 lb. sliced mushroom caps and their stems
1/4 lb. unsalted butter (1stick)
salt and pepper to taste
2 Tbsp. dry vermouth
3 Tbsp. minced Italian parsley
4 Tbsp. Parmesan cheese, freshly grated

1. Slice the mushroom caps, keeping the stems attached. Pre-sliced mushrooms appear quite often in the supermarkets. If you buy them, be sure they are white and not discolored.
2. To a 9-inch skillet, add the mushrooms and 1/2 the butter.
3. Sauté over medium heat for about 5 minutes.
4. As they begin to wilt, season with salt and pepper.
5. Add the vermouth.
6. Sprinkle with the minced parsley, and cook the mushrooms until tender, about 2 minutes.
7. Drain the cooked pasta into a large serving bowl and dot with pieces of the remaining butter to coat the pasta, tossing lightly.
8. Pour the mushroom sauce over the pasta and mix well.
9. Divide the fettuccine into individual bowls and top with the Parmesan cheese.

Some Like it Hot—Sauces with a Kick

Growing up in Greenwich Village was a pretty ordinary affair—pasta wise. My parents were American born and most of the meals from my mother, Catherine's, kitchen were pretty straight forward, fashioned in the American style. Broiled steak, lamb chops, and breaded veal cutlets (which I smeared with ketchup), mashed potatoes, always, with a seasonal vegetable. As a youngster, I ate so many asparagus in springtime, that I vowed never to have them in my kitchen. It was a promise I didn't keep. Catherine's Italian roots surfaced quite often with basil sauces, luscious meat sauces (which we called gravy) a Lasagne now and then, and always Potato Gnocchi and Genoese Ravioli. In fact, as I remember, the word spaghetti covered all the bases in our house. So it was always a treat to have dinner with my Aunt Dora and Uncle Tony. She made all forms of macaroni, which I am still partial to today.

It was not until I changed career directions and started teaching cooking classes that I realized the magnitude of my Italian heritage. Which takes me to sauces with a kick. This gourmet generation is so much more sophisticated and open to new tastes, hence the hot stuff. Adding chiles, red and green peppers, peperoncini, and the kick of cayenne every once in a while adds a new dimension to many old standards.

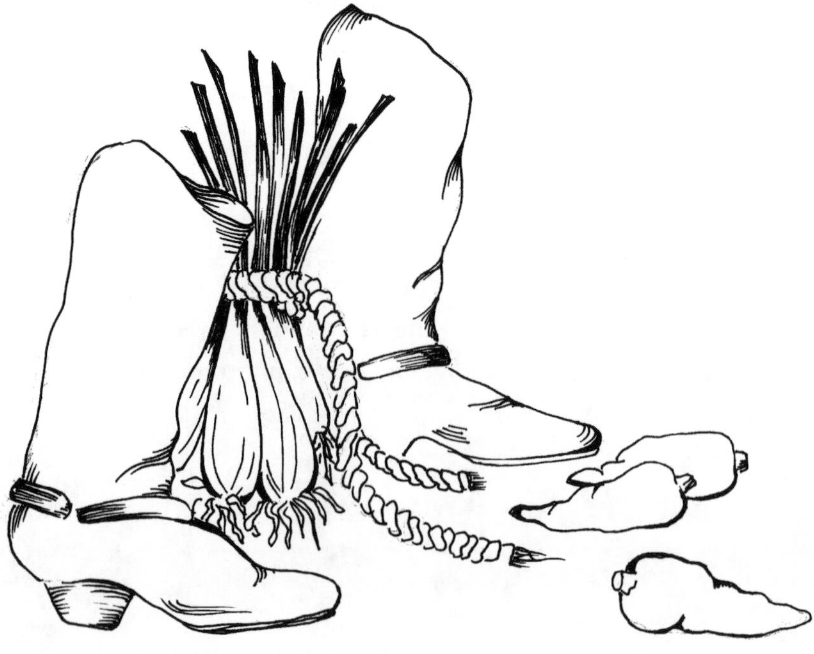

Fra Diavolo Sauce with Linguine

(Serves 4–6)

This sauce gets its kick from garlic, red pepper, and oregano. Cook the pasta while the sauce is simmering. Drain the linguine, pour into a large bowl and then stir in the sauce.

WINE SUGGESTION: Zinfandel

1 lb. Linguini
4 Tbsp. olive oil
2 cloves garlic, minced
1 tsp. crushed red pepper
1/2 tsp. oregano
1 28-oz. can Italian plum tomatoes, coarsely chopped
1 bay leaf
1 Tbsp. finely slivered fresh basil leaves
Salt and freshly ground black pepper

1. In a large skillet or sauté pan, heat the oil.
2. Add the garlic and sauté over medium heat until it softens, but is not browned.
3. Stir in the red pepper, oregano, tomatoes, and bay leaf.
4. Bring to a boil and simmer until the sauce has thickened, about 30 minutes.
5. Stir in the basil, salt and pepper to taste.

Rigatoni all'Arrabbiata

(Serves 6)

Father Hector LaChapelle, an avid cook, graciously shared this recipe with me. He prepares this dish quite often for his pastor, Father Robert Ippolito, and their parishioners.

WINE SUGGESTION: Cabernet Sauvignon

1 lb. Rigatoni
1 oz. dried porcini mushrooms
7 oz. butter
5 oz. pancetta or lean bacon, diced
1–2 dried red chilies, to taste
2 garlic cloves, crushed
8 ripe Italian plum tomatoes, peeled and chopped
fresh basil leaves, torn, plus extra to garnish
2/3 c. freshly grated Parmesan cheese
1/3 c. freshly grated Pecorino cheese

1. Soak the dried mushrooms in warm water to cover for 15–20 minutes.
2. Drain, then squeeze dry with your hands. Finely chop the mushrooms.
3. Melt 4 tablespoons of the butter in a medium saucepan or skillet. Add the pancetta or bacon and stir-fry over medium heat until golden and slightly crispy. Remove the pancetta with a slotted spoon and set it aside.
4. Add the chopped mushrooms to the pan and cook in the same way. Remove and set aside with the pancetta or bacon.
5. Crumble 1 chili into the pan, add the garlic and cook, stirring for a few minutes, until the garlic turns golden.
6. Add the tomatoes and basil and season with salt.
7. Cook gently, stirring occasionally, for 10–15 minutes.
8. Meanwhile, cook the rigatoni in a pan of salted boiling water, according to the instructions on the package.
9. Add the pancetta or bacon and the mushrooms to the tomato sauce.
10. Taste for seasoning, adding more chilies if you prefer a hotter flavor. If the sauce is too dry, stir in a little of the pasta water.

11. Drain the pasta and turn it into a warmed bowl.
12. Dice the remaining butter, add it to the pasta with the cheese, then toss until well coated.
13. Pour the tomato sauce over the pasta, toss well, and serve immediately with a few basil leaves sprinkled on top.

Amatriciana Sauce with Bucatini

(Serves 4–6)

Amatrice is a little town in central Italy, sitting between the Lazio and Abruzzi regions. The recipe varies on either side of the border, but always with delectable results. Pancetta is Italian bacon, which is cured but not smoked. If bacon is used, blanch quickly in boiling water.

WINE SUGGESTION: Zinfandel or Gattinara

1 lb. Bucatini cooked to *al dente*
3 Tbsp. extra-virgin olive oil
2 oz. pancetta or bacon, finely chopped
1 medium onion, finely chopped
2 cloves garlic, minced
1/2 tsp. dried oregano
1 28-oz. can Italian plum tomatoes, coarsely chopped, or diced tomatoes
1/2 tsp. hot red pepper flakes
salt and freshly ground pepper to taste
6 Tbsp. Pecorino Romano cheese

1. In a large skillet or sauté pan, heat 2 tablespoons oil with the pancetta.
2. When the pancetta starts to brown add the onion and garlic and sauté over medium heat.
3. Stir in the oregano, tomatoes, and pepper flakes. Bring to a boil, reduce the heat, and simmer, uncovered, for 20 minutes.
4. Add salt and pepper to taste. Stir in the remaining oil.
5. Sprinkle with the cheese.

Bigoli with Anchovy Sauce

(Serves 2)

My father's favorite dish and Mother didn't mind. She rustled it up in minutes.

WINE SUGGESTION: Barbera d'Asti

1/2 lb. Bigoli
1/4 c. olive oil
2 Tbsp. unsalted butter
2 cloves garlic, minced
1 2-oz. can anchovy fillets, drained
freshly ground pepper to taste

1. In a small skillet, cook the garlic in the olive oil and butter over low heat until the garlic softens.
2. Add the anchovy fillets and sauté gently until the anchovies dissolve.
3. Meanwhile, cook the pasta to *al dente.* Drain and toss with sauce. Add the freshly ground pepper.

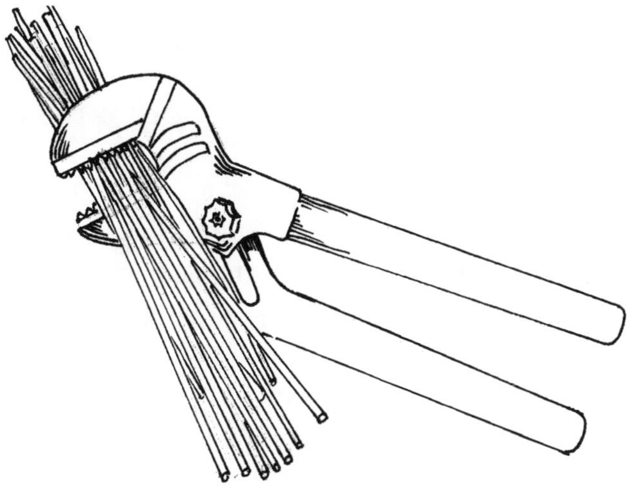

Capellini Capricoiosi
(Spicy Capellini)

(Serves 4–6)

A Lidia Bastianich recipe.

Lidia Bastianich, the First Lady of Italian cuisine in the United States, is dedicated to bringing the best of Italian cooking to the world. Four restaurants, four books, and a television series do not diminish her zest for life. Her books contain hundreds of mouthwatering recipes and information about quality ingredients and regional wines in addition to charming anecdotes and stories of her life in Italy.

Peperoncini, hot pickled peppers, also known as Tuscan peppers, are readily found in the supermarket.

WINE SUGGESTION: Lidia suggests a good chianti with this dish.

1/3 c. olive oil
8 slices bacon, chopped
2 medium onions, thinly sliced
10 peperoncini, drained, seeded and chopped
1 35-oz. can (about 3 cups) crushed Italian tomatoes, drained
1/4 tsp. salt
3/4 c. Parmesan cheese, freshly grated
2 Tbsp. minced Italian flat-leaf parsley (optional)

1. In a large sauté pan, heat 3 tablespoons olive oil over high heat. Add the bacon and cook until lightly browned, about 10 minutes.
2. Add the onions, and cook, stirring occasionally, until golden, about 15 minutes.
3. Add the peperoncini, tomatoes, and salt and simmer about 10 minutes.
4. Meanwhile, bring 4 quarts of water to a boil. Add salt. Add the pasta and cook until *al dente,* about 3 minutes.
5. Drain the pasta and toss it with the remaining oil. Stir in the sauce. Add the cheese, toss and serve immediately garnished with the parsley.

Say Cheese!

I've often wondered why kids love macaroni and cheese so much. Have they tasted a delicious dish of Tagliatelle alla Panna (Tagliatelle with a Cream and Cheese Sauce)? I doubt it. It's easy to conclude, however, that our American Macaroni and Cheese dish, laden with processed cheese and chemical additives, belongs on another planet and not on their plates.

Good quality, imported cheese is of utmost importance in all pasta dishes containing cheese.

A few basic rules to live by:

1. Don't skimp on price.
2. Buy it in one piece, store it in plastic wrap then in foil in the vegetable bin of the refrigerator. Grate when needed.
3. Do not substitute Pecorino for Parmesan. Pecorino Romano is a more pungent cheese that pairs well with more robust sauces.

Pasta Penne with Tomato, Cream, and Five Cheeses

(Serves 8)

Adapted from a recipe by George Germon and Johanne Killeen, authors of *Cucina Simpatica.*

George Germon and Johanne Killeen, husband and wife team and co-owners of Al Forno, their renowned restaurant in Providence, Rhode Island, were educated in the fine arts at the Rhode Island School of Design. His discipline was sculpture and hers photography, but they were destined to make their mark in the restaurant world.

It didn't take long for Al Forno to hit the top of the culinary charts. Al Forno's food is predominantly Italian. The dishes are straightforward, totally original, creative and inventive. "We don't do culinary gymnastics. Young cooks sometimes don't understand simplicity, to make things shine with just three ingredients," says Germon.

If you want to make a splash, have individual ceramic gratin dishes in your stash of dinnerware.

They make an appealing presentation for this recipe.

Wine Suggestion: Bardolino or Soave

1 lb. Penne Rigate
8 ceramic gratin dishes (1 1/2 to 2-cup capacity)

Preheat oven to 500 degrees.

2 c. heavy cream
1 c. canned plum tomatoes, cut in chunks, in heavy purée
1/2 c. Pecorino Romano,(1 1/2 oz.) freshly grated
1/2 c. Italian Fontina (about 1 1/2 oz.)
2 Tbsp. ricotta
4 Tbsp. Gorgonzola, crumbled
4 oz. whole milk mozzarella, grated, shredded, or 2 small fresh mozzarella, sliced (1/4 lb.)
8 fresh basil leaves, chopped (1 1/2 oz.)
4 Tbsp. unsalted butter (1/2 stick)

1. Bring 6 quarts water to a boil. Salt.
2. In a large bowl, combine all the ingredients except the penne and butter. Stir to mix.
3. Cook the pasta for 4 minutes. Drain and add to the mixing bowl, stirring to combine.
4. Divide the pasta among 8 individual ceramic, shallow, gratin dishes. Dot with butter.
5. Place the dishes on baking trays and bake until lightly browned and bubbly, 7–10 minutes.

Penne and Zucchini with an Egg and Cheese Bonus

(Serves 4–6)

Be organized. Have all the ingredients ready to go. Beat the eggs with the cheese and butter. Mince the garlic; slice the onions and the zucchini. Put on the water to boil. Start sautéing. Dinner will be ready in two shakes.

WINE SUGGESTION: Chablis

1 lb. Penne
2 eggs, beaten
4 Tbsp. Pecorino Romano cheese, freshly grated
4 Tbsp. unsalted butter, at room temperature, cut into small pieces
3 Tbsp. olive oil
1 clove garlic, minced
1 large onion, or 3 shallots, sliced thin
2 medium zucchini, sliced into 1/4-inch rounds
1/4 tsp. dried thyme
1/4 tsp. red pepper flakes
salt and freshly ground pepper to taste

1. In a large bowl, beat the eggs. Add the cheese and butter. Mix well.
2. Bring six quarts water to a boil. Add the salt. Cook the penne according to the package instructions.
3. Meanwhile, in a 12-inch skillet or sauté pan, add the oil. When it hazes over, add the onion and cook until the onion or shallots become translucent and soft, but not colored, about 8 minutes.
4. Add the garlic. Sauté 1 minute.
5. Add the zucchini and cook over high heat, with stirring, for 3–4 minutes.
6. Stir in the thyme, red pepper and salt, and freshly ground pepper.
7. Drain the penne into the bowl containing the egg/cheese/butter mixture and stir.
8. Mix in the zucchini and serve immediately. Pass additional cheese if desired.

Fettuccine alla Carbonara
(Fettuccine with Egg and Bacon Sauce)

(Serves 4–6)

There are so many versions of this dish that only the name remains the same. Smoked hog jowls and strips of salt pork, happily, are displaced by pancetta, Italian cured bacon, or bacon.

WINE SUGGESTION: Bardolino

1 lb. Fettuccine
4 Tbsp. unsalted butter, softened and at room temperature
2 large eggs
2 egg yolks
1 c. Parmesan cheese, freshly grated
8 slices bacon, or 1/4 lb. pancetta, finely chopped
1/2 c. heavy cream
lots of freshly ground black pepper

1. In a small bowl, beat the eggs and yolks with a whisk.
2. Stir in 1/2 cup Parmesan cheese, salt, and freshly ground pepper to taste.
3. In a large skillet or sauté pan, over moderate heat, cook the bacon or pancetta until crisp.
4. Pour off almost all the fat. Stir in the cream and keep it at a simmer. Grind in the pepper.
5. Meanwhile, cook the pasta to *al dente.* Drain and remove to a large bowl. Coat the pasta with the softened butter.
6. Add the pasta to the skillet containing the simmering bacon/cream mixture.
7. Add the egg/cheese mixture and stir thoroughly. The heat of the pasta and the other ingredients will cook the raw eggs on contact.
8. Sprinkle the remaining cheese on the individual portions.

Pesto and Goat Cheese Sauce

(Enough for 1/2–3/4 lbs. Pasta)

This sauce works well with Potato Gnocchi (recipe in Section IV). The goat cheese has a bit of a bite and once again the green basil makes for a pleasing presentation.

Wine Suggestion: Barolo

2 c. fresh basil, washed and towel-dried
1/3 c. olive oil
salt to taste
4 Tbsp. goat cheese
freshly ground pepper to taste

1. Put the basil in a food processor or blender and process briefly.
2. Add the oil in a steady stream. Add the salt and blend until smooth.
3. Transfer the mixture to a bowl and stir in the goat cheese. Mix until smooth.
4. Add 1 or 2 tablespoons of the boiling water from the gnocchi to the sauce.
5. Toss with gnocchi.

Gorgonzola Sauce

(Enough for 1/2–3/4 lbs. Pasta)

If you haven't set your sights on a sauce for Ricotta Gnocchi, try this recipe if you want to make a high caloric definitive statement. I love it with Farfalle or Fusilli too.

WINE SUGGESTION: Cabernet Sauvignon

4 Tbsp. unsalted butter
6 oz. Gorgonzola cheese, crumbled.
1 c. heavy cream
freshly ground white pepper to taste
3/4 cup freshly grated Parmesan cheese

1. In a medium saucepan, melt the butter over moderate heat.
2. Add the gorgonzola with stirring.
3. When the cheese has melted, add the cream.
4. Simmer over low heat and cook 4–5 minutes. The sauce should be thick enough to coat the back of a spoon.
5. Grind in the pepper and stir in the Parmesan.
6. Stir the sauce into the pasta and serve immediately.

Creamy Garlic and Mushroom Sauce

(Serves 4 as appetizer)

Serve with fresh fettuccine or cheese tortellini

A word about garlic: be brave. Banish the garlic press unless you are making a marinade. The press releases too much oil from the cloves. To retain garlic's true flavor, cut or mince by hand using a sharp knife. Garlic bulbs should be stored in a cool, dark place.

WINE SUGGESTION: Soave

1/2 oz. dry porcini, soaked in 1 cup warm water for 1/2 hour. Remove the porcini and coarsely chop. Strain and reserve the liquid.
4 cloves garlic, minced using a sharp knife or cleaver
3 Tbsp. unsalted butter
8 oz. white button mushrooms, sliced thin
3 Tbsp. Marsala wine
1 c. heavy cream or half and half
1/4 tsp. dry thyme
salt and freshly ground pepper to taste
3/4 c. freshly grated Parmesan cheese

1. In a large sauté pan or skillet, cook the garlic over low heat for 3 minutes. Do not let the garlic brown.
2. Add the porcini and sliced mushrooms. Raise heat to medium. Cook, with stirring, for 3–4 minutes.
3. Add the reserved porcini liquid and Marsala and cook 3 minutes.
4. Add the cream or half and half, thyme, salt, and pepper and cook over medium heat, stirring occasionally, for about 10 minutes.
5. Add the Parmesan, stir, and cook 5 minutes.
6. Cook the pasta to *al dente,* drain, and toss with the sauce. Add additional cheese if desired.

Eat Your Veggies—Vegetable Sauces and Dishes

Basil: King of the realm

The cook's aphrodisiac and a friend for all seasons

Since these recipes focus on vegetables, it seemed like a good spot to talk about one of my favorite herbs: basil. Basil is an aromatic herb and a relative to mint. It was used in Greek kitchens as early as 400 B.C. In India, it was used primarily in religious ceremonies and funerals. Egyptians combined it with other medicinal materials to embalm their dead. And as Keats lamented in his poem, *Isabella,* her murdered lover's head was preserved in a pot of basil. Thankfully, the Romans chose to equate basil with jasmine and the rose as symbols for lovers.

Basil thrives in Genoa on the Ligurian coast of Italy. So many dishes in Genoa's cuisine rely on this pungent herb's ability to transform a recipe from the ordinary to the exceptional. In early days, the Genoese were territorial about their treasure but they couldn't keep basil under wraps forever. Happily, it aggressively found its way into the cuisines of many cultures.

I am terribly partial to its addictive fragrance because it transports me to another time and place. Basil was a commonplace ingredient in my mother's kitchen. It was a necessary addition to her minestrone soup, tomato and meat sauces, and best of all, served as the basis for her incomparable pesto sauce. I have no idea why she never added pine nuts to her pesto. Parmigiano-Reggiano was her cheese of choice. Pecorino Romano, deemed *too pungent,* wasn't allowed to sidle up to the King of Cheeses. She adamantly insisted that if one clove of garlic was allowed in, it must make its way from the mortar and pestle, not the garlic press.

My mother's culinary decree wasn't far off the mark. Geographical research has borne her out. Genoa's proximity to France, the land of butter and delicate flavors, greatly influenced Genoese cooking and my mother. Sweet butter was queen in her kitchen and dominated much of her cooking. I firmly believe it's a "trickle-down" regional factor from her generation to mine. But I've become more broad-minded. I add a clove of finely minced garlic to my pesto sauce, but pignoli are still not allowed in. I replace them with cream cheese for substance and sweetness and to further entice my pesto sauce to cling to sturdy strands of fettuccine.

Basil Facts:

Basil is the tomato's best friend and soul mate. When I lived on Long Island and a garden was not in my realm, all the basil bouquets that graced my windowsill were generously picked from my friend Sally Vuillet's garden. She abandoned the greenhouse where her magnificent orchids bloomed so profusely in the dead of winter, to plant a patch of sweet basil in summer. By summer's end, the basil plants stood tall, ready to flavor a sauce made from her husband Bob's succulent tomatoes.

Basil enhances chicken, meat, fish, pasta, gnocchi, salads, and vegetables. Because it's such a delicate herb, belying its pungent aroma and predominant flavor, tear it rather than chop it. Add basil to the pot the last five minutes of cooking because too much heat destroys its sweet flavor.

To Freeze or Not to Freeze:

Simply said, a basil leaf will succumb in the freezer and turn black unless married with olive oil and salt. It's an easy kitchen exercise. Put freshly washed and towel-dried basil leaves in the bowl of a food processor or blender with extra-virgin olive oil and salt and mix at high speed until evenly blended. *Garlic and cheese are not added now. Add these ingredients later to the defrosted basil/oil/salt mixture.* Spoon the mixture into small baggies, seal, fold in half, and stash in the freezer. The vibrant green color is maintained and the beginning of a pesto sauce is there for the asking with a mere snip of the scissors. When ready to use, slit the baggie, pop out the frozen basil mixture, and transfer to a medium bowl. It will defrost in a matter of minutes. Add the garlic, cheese, and pine nuts (if you wish) to the defrosted basil/oil/salt mixture.

My Mother's Pesto Sauce, Amended

(Serves 4–6)

WINE SUGGESTION: Chardonnay

1 lb. Linguine
2 c. fresh basil leaves, moderately packed
1/2 c. extra-virgin olive oil
1 clove garlic, peeled and crushed with the blade of a heavy knife
1/2 tsp. salt
3 Tbsp. softened, unsalted butter
3 oz. cream cheese
1/2 cup Parmigiano-Reggiano

1. Put the basil, oil, garlic, and salt in a food processor or blender. Mix at high speed until evenly blended.
2. Transfer the mixture to a bowl, and using a fork, beat in the butter, cream cheese, and Parmesan cheese.
3. Bring a large pot of water to a boil. Salt. Blend in 3 tablespoons of the hot water from the pasta pot to lighten the pesto sauce. Cook the linguine in ample amounts of salted water until *al dente.*
4. Drain the pasta and transfer to a large bowl. Stir in the pesto sauce.
5. Serve in individual bowls and pass the Parmigiano.

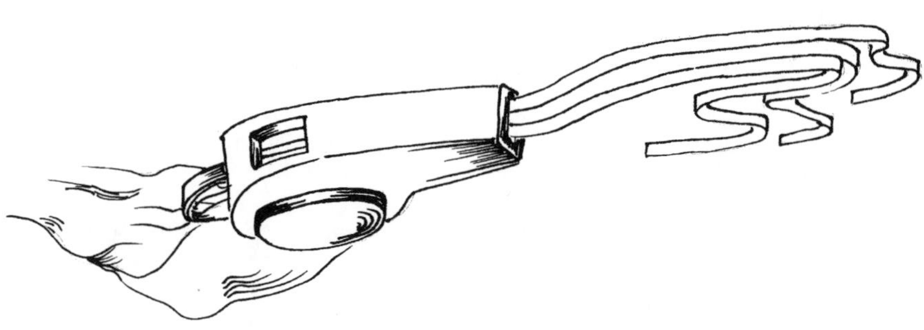

Pasta Primavera

(Serves 4–6)

There has been an on-going feud between Arrigo Cipriani, the proprietor of Harry's Bar on Calle Vallaresso in Venice and Sirio Maccioni, the owner of the renowned Le Cirque restaurant in Manhattan. Each claims to be the originator of the recipe for Pasta Primavera. These restaurateurs may not be able to settle their gastronomic dispute, but we win either way. Harry's Bar serves these springtime vegetables with pasta. The dish is laden with shiitake mushrooms, artichokes, zucchini, asparagus, and tomatoes, but the dish is always dependent on seasonal vegetables. Sirio includes broccoli, green beans, and peas in his creation.

I chose the vegetables I like best and you can too. It will be your very own version of Pasta Primavera.

WINE SUGGESTION: Soave

1 lb. Spaghetti cooked to *al dente*

The vegetables can be prepared up to 24 hours ahead and refrigerated.

4 Tbsp. olive oil
1 clove garlic, minced
8 oz. mushrooms, shiitake or button, caps only, thinly sliced
2 artichoke hearts, canned in water, drained, and cut into thin slices
1 small onion, finely chopped
4 small zucchini, cut into 1/4-inch dice
1 lb. asparagus, tough ends discarded, cut into 1-inch lengths, refreshed in cold water
3 plum tomatoes cut into quarter-inch dice
salt and freshly ground pepper

1. In a large skillet, heat the oil over medium heat. Add the garlic and cook 30 seconds.
2. Add the mushrooms and cook, with stirring, until softened, and the liquid has evaporated, about 5 minutes.
3. Add the onion, cook about 5 minutes.

4. Add the zucchini, asparagus, and tomatoes. Add salt and pepper to taste.
5. Cook with stirring for 10 minutes or until the vegetables are just cooked.

For the Sauce:

4 Tbsp. unsalted butter
1/2 c. heavy cream
2/3 c. Parmesan cheese, freshly grated
salt and freshly ground pepper to taste

1. In a pot large enough to hold the drained pasta and all the vegetables, melt the butter over medium heat.
2. Add the cream and cheese and stir constantly until heated through.
3. Reduce the heat and add the vegetables and spaghetti to the sauce. Correct for seasonings. If the sauce seems too dry, add a little cream, but it should not be soupy. Serve immediately.

Penne in an Artichoke Porcini Sauce

(Serves 6)

Nanette Pizzi served this delicious pasta dish to us when we visited her in Milan. The dinner capped off a delightful day touring this ancient, but oh-so-modern Italian city. When we stopped at the local outdoor market, Nanette chose a dozen or so small artichokes for the sauce she would prepare for that evening's meal. Watching her as she deftly cleaned the artichokes, I couldn't help thinking how comfortable Italians are in the kitchen. I smiled, too, at some of the shortcuts Nanette took in the preparation of this scrumptious dish. We'll take all of them and add one—prepared artichoke hearts packed in water.

WINE SUGGESTION: Valpolicella

1 lb. Penne or Penette, smooth not ridged
4 Tbsp. unsalted butter (1/2 stick)
4 Tbsp. olive oil
1 medium onion, chopped fine
2 14.5-oz. cans artichoke hearts, packed in water, quartered vertically
1 clove garlic, minced
1/2 cup dry white wine or dry vermouth
1/2 oz. dried porcini soaked in hot water for 30 minutes. Remove and coarsely chop the porcini.
1 14.5-oz. low-salt canned chicken broth
1 14.5-oz. can diced tomatoes
2 Tbsp. minced Italian flat-leaf parsley
salt and freshly ground pepper to taste
2 Tbsp. unsalted butter at room temperature
Parmigiano Reggiano, freshly grated

1. In a large sauté pan, melt the butter with the oil over moderate heat.
2. Add the onion and sauté until limp, about 10 minutes.
3. Add the artichokes and garlic. Sauté 3 minutes.

4. Add the wine or vermouth. Allow the alcohol to dissipate, about 2 minutes.
5. Add the porcini and 1 cup of the chicken broth.
6. Add the tomatoes and parsley.
7. Cover and simmer over low heat for about 50 minutes. Add more broth as needed.
8. While the sauce is cooking, bring a large pot of water to a boil. Add salt and cook the pasta to *al dente.*
9. Drain the pasta into a large bowl and swirl in the softened butter. Stir in the sauce.
10. Serve in individual bowls and top with the Parmesan cheese.

Angel Hair Pasta Wrapped in Eggplant

(Serves 8)

Linda King Jannuzzi, a graduate of the CIA, makes this recipe whenever her friends cry out for some Italian comfort food.

WINE SUGGESTION: Pinot Grigio

Preheat oven to 350 degrees.

Sauce:

6 Tbsp. extra-virgin olive oil
1 lb. red onions, finely chopped
1 28-oz. + 1 14-oz. cans diced tomatoes
Salt and freshly ground pepper
15 large sprigs of Italian parsley, leaves only, chopped fine (about 1/2 cup loosely packed).
5 large basil leaves, torn into thirds

1. In a large sauté pan, heat oil over medium heat.
2. Add onions and sauté for 5 minutes.
3. Add tomatoes, lower heat, cover, and cook for 20 minutes, stirring occasionally.
4. Season to taste with salt and pepper. Add parsley and basil and mix well. Cook 5 to 10 minutes more to reduce sauce.
5. Set aside for the assembly.

For the eggplant:

2 eggplants at 1+ pound each
Coarse salt
2 c. vegetable oil
1 c. all purpose flour

1. Peel and cut eggplants into vertical slices, 1/4-inch thick (16 slices total).
2. Salt slices and place on parchment paper-lined trays for 1 hour.
3. Rinse slices and pat dry with paper towels.

4. In a large skillet, heat the oil over moderate heat.
5. Lightly flour the slices and fry a few at a time until golden on both sides, then transfer to paper towels to remove excess oil.

Assembly ingredients:

1/2 lb. Angel hair pasta, cooked to *al dente.*
Sauce
Eggplant
Basil leaves
1 c. grated mozzarella cheese
1 c. freshly grated Parmigiano-Reggiano

Assembly:

1. Mix pasta with 2 cups of prepared sauce in a bowl.
2. Lay the eggplant slices on a work surface. Spoon 1/3 cup of the pasta mixture on each slice of eggplant with a few sprinkles of basil leaves.
3. Roll the eggplant around the pasta.
4. Place rolls in an oiled oven-proof baking dish.
5. Sprinkle with shredded mozzarella and Parmesan cheese.
6. Pour 1 cup of the remaining sauce down middle of the rolls
7. Bake at 350 degrees until rolls are warm and cheese is melted (about 10 to 15 minutes).
8. Serve 2 rolls per person with basil leaves and extra sauce as a garnish.

Pan-Fried Zucchini Blossoms

(Makes 16)

Zucchini blossoms are hard to find, unless you have a friendly gardener who is willing to let you raid his zucchini patch. When we lived in New York, our friend Bob Vuillet, a Master Vegetable Gardener, cultivated a huge garden of eggplant, tomatoes, beans, onions, and zucchini. Of course, you know there is no such thing as a few zucchini, so Bob's zucchini crop found its way around the neighborhood. But only my husband Rudy got the prize pick of the crop—zucchini blossoms. When we traveled in Italy, from Lake Como to the Amalfi coast, Rudy always managed to find zucchini blossoms on the menu. If not, he would cajole the chef into preparing this delicate vegetable. Italian chefs in the little trattorias in the countryside are always anxious to comply with any food request, especially if an American can speak Italian.

Italians are masters at frying and have proven that a fried vegetable need not be soggy or heavy. Properly fried, the delicate, golden zucchini blossom can star as the centerpiece in an antipasto platter or they can be served in tandem with other vegetables.

16 zucchini blossoms
1 c. flour
1 c. water
1 c. vegetable oil
Kosher salt and freshly ground pepper

1. Trim the stems from the flowers and remove the pistils in the center of each zucchini blossom. Cut the blossoms so they lay flat.
2. In a small bowl, add the flour to the water, to make a thin batter.
3. Wash each flower in cold water and dry on paper towels.
4. Heat the oil in a medium skillet over medium high heat.
5. Dip each flower into the batter, and fry in batches, a few at a time, until they're crisp and golden, about 1–2 minutes per side.
6. Remove blossoms with a slotted spoon and place onto paper towels. Season with salt and pepper.

Section III

The Sea's Bounty

Italy is surrounded by the Adriatic, Ionian, Mediterranean, Tyrrhenian, and Ligurian Seas. It's no wonder that fish and shellfish play starring roles in Italian cuisine. Of course, so many varieties found in Italy's waters are not available here in the United States, but we do have good clams, great crab, succulent lobsters, decent mussels, (if you can harvest them from the waters in your area), giant sea scallops, and sweet little bays. Good quality salmon, cod, flounder, mahi-mahi, grouper, and pompano are all available in high-end supermarkets and good fish stores. Everything from the sea marries well with pasta.

Calamari (Squid) in Tomato Sauce

(Serves 4–6)

Years ago, whenever I made my husband, Rudy's, favorite pasta dish, calamari in a tomato sauce served over linguine, the reviews were often mixed. Rudy's criticism usually surfaced as "the calamari are tough. Perhaps you cooked them too long. My father only cooks them for a couple of minutes." To some degree, Rudy's observation was an astute one. The calamari were tough. In reality, I didn't cook them long enough. Mistakenly, I followed my father-in-law Gino's, fried *calamari cooking time when I made my calamari tomato sauce. Wrong.*

The problem was solved when I had the good fortune to meet a man in one of Marcella Hazan's classes who owned a wholesale fish market in Florida. When I told him of my calamari plight, he said, "That's easy. Simmer the squid in the sauce for 15 minutes, covered. Then continue to cook for another 15 minutes with the cover off." Now, I always get great calamari reviews from my own candid critic.

Tender squid are 1 inch wide and have a stomach about 3 inches long. If your fishmonger can't supply you with fresh squid, cleaned calamari, tubes (bodies), and tentacles can also be found frozen in 2 1/2-lb. packages.

Thaw the squid in the refrigerator or in cold running water and drain in a colander. Transfer to a platter lined with paper towels to absorb excess moisture. Pat dry. Cut the bodies of the squid horizontally into 1/2-inch rings. Cut the tentacles lengthwise if they are large.

WINE SUGGESTION: Verdicchio

1 lb. Linguine
1/4 c. olive oil
2 Tbsp. unsalted butter
1 medium onion, minced
1/3 c. dry white wine or dry vermouth
2 Tbsp. minced Italian flat-leaf parsley
2 8-oz. cans tomato sauce
salt and freshly ground pepper to taste
2 1/2 lbs. squid, cleaned and cut as described

1. In a large skillet, sauté the onion in the oil/butter over moderate heat until soft but not brown.
2. Add the wine or vermouth. Raise the heat to high to boil off the alcohol, about 1 minute.
3. Add the parsley, tomato sauce, and salt and pepper to taste.
4. Stir in the squid, cover, and simmer gently for 15 minutes. Remove the cover and simmer an additional 15 minutes.
5. Cook the linguine to *al dente.* Drain the pasta and transfer to a bowl. Spoon the sauce and some squid over the pasta and stir to mix. Top the individual portions with the remaining calamari.

Rudy's White Clam Sauce for Linguine

(Serves 4–6)

Opening fresh clams can be an exercise in futility. However, two approaches can ease the frustration. Put the clams in the freezer for a couple of hours. Then, a clam or sharp paring knife easily slips into the partially-separated shell. Alternatively, gently steam them in a pot with a bottle of clam juice. They open beautifully. Reserve the juice. If fresh clams are unavailable, substitute canned clams. Use 2 6 1/2-ounce cans of chopped or minced clams. The luscious flavor of fresh clams, however, takes this dish to another level.

WINE SUGGESTION: Soave

1 lb. Linguine
3 dozen littleneck or cherrystone clams, washed and scrubbed
1/4 c. olive oil
1 small onion, finely chopped
4 garlic cloves, peeled and finely chopped
1/4 c. dry white wine or dry vermouth
1 bottle clam juice, if needed
salt and freshly ground pepper, to taste
2 Tbsp. unsalted butter
2 Tbsp. minced Italian flat-leaf parsley

1. Shuck the clams over a strainer set in a bowl to retain the liquid. Coarsely chop the clams. Set aside.
2. Strain the liquid from the clams through a double layer of wet cheesecloth or paper coffee filter to remove any remaining sand.
3. Measure 1 1/2 cups of the juice from the shucked clams. Add additional bottled clam juice if the fresh clams don't have enough juice. Set aside.
4. In a large sauté pan, heat the olive oil over medium heat until it glazes over. Add the onion and sauté until translucent, about 5 minutes.
5. Turn the heat to low, add the garlic, and sauté until soft, about 2 minutes. Take care not to burn the garlic.
6. Add the wine or vermouth.

7. Pour in the reserved clam liquid. Raise the heat to medium and cook until the liquid is somewhat reduced, about 6 minutes.
8. Reduce the heat to low. Add the chopped clams and butter and cook until the butter melts, about 2 minutes. Season with salt and freshly ground pepper. Stir in the parsley and remove from the heat.
9. Meanwhile, cook the pasta to *al dente* and drain into a large bowl. Stir in the clam sauce, reserving about 1/4 of the sauce. Divide the pasta into separate bowls and garnish with the reserved clam sauce.

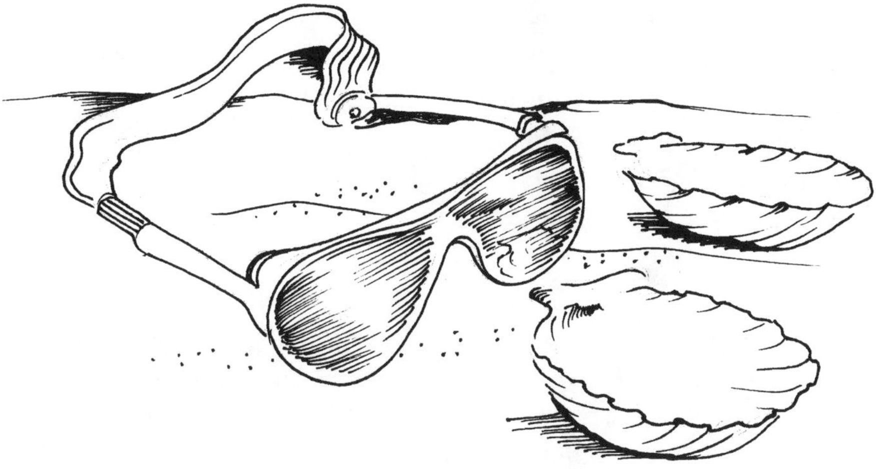

Nina's Shrimp Scampi with Campanile

(Serves 4–6)

WINE SUGGESTION: Pinot Blanc

1 lb. Campanile, a bell-shaped pasta

My daughter Nina and her husband, Paul, declare that extra-large shrimp and lots of garlic are critical to the success of this dish. They leave the tail shell intact because it lessens the amount of curl and makes for an attractive presentation.

1 lb. extra large shrimp, peeled and deveined, leaving tail shell intact.
6 Tbsp. unsalted butter, at room temperature
2 Tbsp. extra virgin olive oil
3/4 c. dry vermouth or dry white wine
1 medium onion, chopped fine
4 cloves garlic, sliced thin
1 Tbsp. minced Italian flat-leaf parsley
salt and freshly ground pepper to taste

1. In a chef's pan or large sauté pan, melt 2 tablespoons butter with 2 tablespoons oil over moderate heat.
2. Add the onion and sauté until it becomes translucent, about 8 minutes.
3. Reduce the heat to low and add the garlic. Cook until it softens but does not brown.

4. Turn the heat to medium, add the vermouth or wine. Cook until the sauce reduces and the alcohol has dissipated.
5. Meanwhile bring a large pot of water to a boil. Add the salt and pasta and cook to *al dente.*
6. While the pasta is cooking, sauté the shrimp over medium heat, turning several times until the shrimp turn pink, about 4 minutes. Be careful not to overcook the shrimp.
7. Add the pasta to the sauce and toss to mix. Add the remaining butter and salt and pepper to taste. Sprinkle with the parsley and serve immediately.

Mussels (Cozze)

My love affair with mussels began on a trip to Venice where Venetians have their pick, wild or farm raised. Here in the States, however, mussels gathered from the sea are hard to find. As a teenager, my son, Johnny Gambarelli, never let the opportunity pass to go mussel hunting in Long Island Sound. I guess the three-generation apple hasn't fallen far from the tree.

Cleaning mussels is a laborious task, but he never walked away. Each one must be scrubbed and de-bearded under cold running water. Finally, the mussels are transferred to a large bowl of water containing a few tablespoons of cornmeal. The hope is that the irritant will help spew out any remaining sand. The cleaning process is then complete.

Johnny moved out and got married. I buy farm raised mussels.

Plan to cook the mussels the day you buy them. Put them in a bowl of cold water and discard those that float or are cracked. There should be few rejects.

Johnny's Quick Mussel Sauce for Spaghetti

(Serves 4–6)

WINE SUGGESTION: Pinot Grigio

Mussels with pasta are a delicious recipe alternative to clams in the summertime. Johnny and his wife, Lynn, maintain that they adapt easily to the casualness of al fresco dining. When you serve this dish, be sure to have a good loaf of Italian or French bread to soak up the wonderful juices.

1 lb. Spaghetti
5 lbs. mussels, cleaned as described
4 Tbsp. olive oil
1 small onion, minced
1/4 c. minced Italian flat-leaf parsley
2 Tbsp. minced fresh basil or 1 Tbsp. dried
2 cloves garlic, minced
1/2 c. dry white wine or dry vermouth
salt and freshly ground pepper to taste

1. In a large pot equipped with a tight-fitting cover, warm the oil over moderate heat. Add all the ingredients except the mussels and pasta and cook over moderately high heat for about 3 to 4 minutes.
2. Add the mussels, cover and cook until the mussels open, about 5 minutes. Be sure to stir with a large spoon once or twice. Discard any that do not open.
3. Meanwhile, cook the pasta to *al dente.*
4. Remove the mussels to a large bowl with a slotted spoon. Drain the pasta and add to the mussel broth. Toss to blend.
5. Portion the pasta and serve the mussels in individual bowls.
6. Pass the bread.

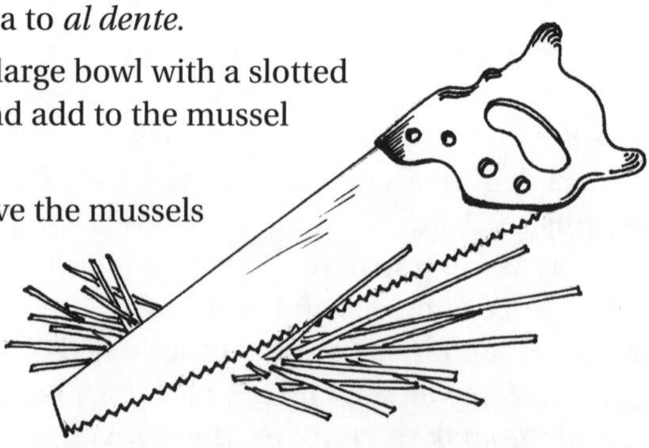

Penne with Seared Sea Scallops and Asparagus in a Basil Sauce

(Serves 2)

Georges Bank, in New England, is home to the most prolific scallop beds on the coast. Not too long ago, however, the government imposed a moratorium on scallop fishing because of their high mortality rate. Smart fishermen took the problem to the Center for Marine and Science Technology at the University of Massachusetts. The scientists discovered that because the scallops were so abundant, they were literally suffocating themselves. The restrictions were removed and the fishermen declare: "It's like taking candy from a baby."

The ultra fresh scallops, caught the last day out at sea, are sold to upscale restaurants and fancy food purveyors. The remainder of the catch is frozen and sold to supermarkets and specialty shops.

WINE SUGGESTION: Chardonnay

1/4 lb. Penne
1 Tbsp. olive oil
1 Tbsp. unsalted butter
2 shallots, chopped fine
6 asparagus
6 small mushrooms or 4 large, sliced
1/4 c. dry white wine or dry vermouth
salt and freshly ground pepper
2 Tbsp. unsalted butter
1/2 lb. sea scallops, cut in half on the horizontal
3 Tbsp. whipped cream cheese
1/2 c. packed fresh basil leaves, minced

1. Snap off the tough bottoms of the asparagus. Cut in 1/2-inch lengths, then in half vertically. Set aside.
2. Slice the mushrooms. Cut the sea scallops in half horizontally.
3. In a small bowl, mix the basil and cream cheese.
4. In a large non-stick skillet, heat the oil and butter over moderate heat. Add the shallots and asparagus and sauté until the asparagus are cooked but still firm.

5. Add the mushrooms and wine and stir to dissipate the alcohol. Turn off the heat.
6. Choose another skillet that is not non-stick (searing is better accomplished in a stainless steel pan). Heat 2 tablespoons butter and add the sea scallops in a single layer.
7. Raise the heat to high and turn once when one side is seared. Sear the other side. Do not overcook the scallops.
8. Meanwhile, cook the penne to *al dente* in an ample amount of boiling water. Add salt.
9. In a large bowl, toss the penne with the basil sauce and scallops and serve immediately.

Vermicelli with Crabmeat in a Tomato-Cream Sauce

(Serves 4–6)

Fresh crabmeat is essential to the success of this recipe. Don't be tempted to buy pasteurized crab. The taste of the sea, so indispensable to this dish, would be compromised.

Do not add the crab until the last minute, because it becomes tough if overcooked.

This is your chance to use the Basic Tomato Sauce you have stashed in the freezer. The addition of vodka gives this recipe an extra kick.

WINE SUGGESTION: Soave

1 lb. Vermicelli
1 1/2 c. Basic Tomato Sauce I (recipe in Section II)
2 Tbsp. minced Italian flat-leaf parsley
6 Tbsp. heavy cream or half and half
1/4 c. vodka
1 lb. fresh lump crabmeat, picked over to remove any cartilage.

1. Start cooking the pasta.
2. In a large sauté pan, heat the sauce.
3. Stir in the parsley, cream, and vodka. Simmer, uncovered, about 3 minutes.
4. Stir in the crabmeat and immediately remove from the heat.
5. Drain the pasta into the pan. Toss and serve immediately.

Spinach Fettuccine with Smoked Salmon

(Serves 4–6)

Salmon lovers, this elegant recipe was made especially for you because it's simple and easy to prepare. The green fettuccine is a perfect backdrop for the pink salmon color of the sauce.

WINE SUGGESTION: Pinot Grigio

3/4 lb. spinach Fettuccine
2 Tbsp. unsalted butter
2 Tbsp. finely chopped onion
4 oz. smoked salmon
7 oz. light cream or half and half
freshly grated black pepper

1. In a small skillet, melt the butter.
2. Add the onion and sauté over medium heat until translucent, about 3 minutes.
3. Take 1/2 of the salmon and roughly chop.
4. Add the salmon and cream to the skillet and cook over low heat for about 5 minutes.
5. Using a blender or food processor, process the mixture until well blended.
6. Cut the remaining salmon into 1/2-inch strips. Set aside.
7. Bring a large pot of water to a boil. Salt the water. Cook the fettuccine to *al dente. Dry fettuccine cooks in about 3 minutes.* Drain the pasta and turn it into a large mixing bowl.
8. Stir in the sauce and toss to mix. Add the pepper.
9. Gently stir in the reserved salmon strips and serve immediately.

Lasagne di Mare (*Shellfish Lasagne*)

(Serves 4–6)

Father La Chapelle makes fresh pasta for this ethereal seafood lasagne.

WINE SUGGESTION: Pinot Grigio

6–8 fresh egg lasagna sheets
4–6 sea scallops
1 lb. peeled raw shrimp
1 garlic clove, minced
6 Tbsp. unsalted butter
1/2 c. flour
2 1/2 c. hot milk
1/2 c. heavy cream
1/2 c. dry white wine
1 envelope saffron powder
pinch cayenne pepper
4 1/2 oz. Fontina cheese, thinly sliced
1 c. Parmesan cheese, freshly grated
salt and freshly ground black pepper to taste

Preheat oven to 375 degrees.

1. Cut the scallops and shrimp into bite-size pieces and spread out in a dish. Sprinkle with the garlic and salt and pepper.
2. In a medium saucepan, melt 2 tablespoons butter. Add the scallops and shrimp and toss over medium heat, 1–2 minutes or until the shrimp turn pink. Using a slotted spoon, remove the shellfish to a plate and set aside.
3. Add the remaining butter to the pan and melt over low heat.
4. Sprinkle in the flour and cook, with stirring, for 1–2 minutes. Increase the heat to medium and add the milk a little at a time, whisking after each addition. Bring to a boil and cook, stirring, until the sauce is smooth and very thick.
5. Whisk in the cream, wine, saffron powder, cayenne, and salt and pepper to taste. Remove the sauce from the heat.

6. Spread about a third of the sauce over the bottom of a baking dish.
7. Arrange a layer of lasagne noodles on the sauce.
8. Place half the Fontina slices over the noodles and sprinkle with about a third of the Parmesan cheese.
9. Scatter about half the shellfish evenly on top, then cover with half the lasagna sheets. Repeat the layers, and then cover with the remaining sauce and Parmesan.
10. Bake the lasagne for 30–40 minutes or until the topping is golden brown and bubbling. Let stand for 10 minutes before serving.

Section IV

Do-it-Yourself Dough

The pasta machine was king on all the cooking shows a few years ago, and cookbook authors were attempting to describe the intricacies of hand-mixing, stretching, and rolling out the delicate dough. It was not an easy task.

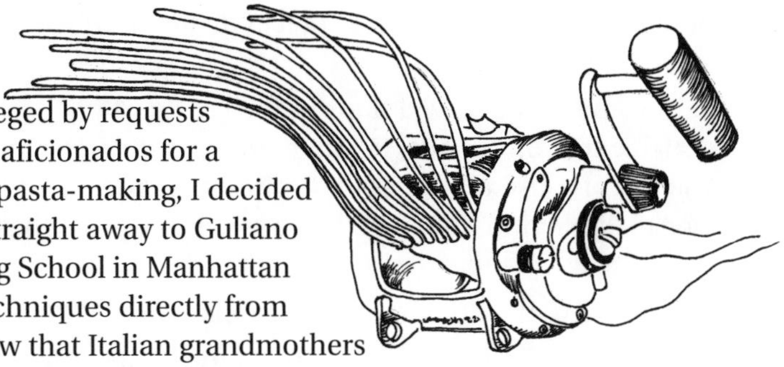

When I was besieged by requests from fresh pasta aficionados for a cooking class in pasta-making, I decided I had better go straight away to Guliano Bugialli's Cooking School in Manhattan to learn pasta techniques directly from the master. I knew that Italian grandmothers made their pasta dough by simply dumping flour on a board, making a well with an egg in the center of the mound, adding salt and oil, and incorporating the flour until "it doesn't take anymore." This was a vague cooking statement, originating perhaps with a person who chose not to share a recipe. So when Guliano instructed us to put 2 cups of flour on a board, I wondered why he was taking us back in time. After all, this is the twenty-first century where ingredients are mixed in bowls. It didn't take long to realize that our deft grandmothers had the right idea. The first class was a daunting experience. Of course, some flour walls came tumbling down at first try, but eventually the soft mass miraculously came together, ready to be kneaded and stretched with the pasta machine.

Fresh Pasta

2 c. unbleached flour
2 extra-large eggs
2 tsp. olive oil
pinch of salt

1. Put the flour in a mound on a board. Using one of the eggs, make a well in the center of the flour forming a circular wall.
2. Break the eggs into the well you've made in the flour, along with the oil and salt. Break up the egg yolks with a fork and using the fork, incorporate the flour from the inner edges of the well, a little at a time. When the batter has amassed enough flour and becomes a dough, clean off the fork and your hands.
3. Scrape up all the flour (a pastry scraper is an invaluable tool for the pasta or bread maker) and pass it through a sieve onto a corner of the board. This step is important before you start the kneading process. You need to rid the remaining flour of the dried globules of dough before you incorporate additional flour. Dried pieces of dough will make holes in the delicate finished product.
4. Take some of the sieved flour to the center of the board and knead the dough with your hands, taking flour from the bottom, a little at a time. You will not use all the flour. Continue to knead, adding flour until "it won't take anymore." When the dough is as soft as a baby's bottom, wrap in plastic wrap and allow to rest up to 1 hour.
5. Cut off 1/3 of the dough, cover the remainder.
6. Working with 1 piece at a time, form the dough into a rectangle. Set the pasta machine at #1, the widest setting. Pass the dough through, then trifold the extruded dough into a package, as you would a letter. Place an open end of the folded dough through the machine on the same setting. Repeat this process for about 6 times, dusting with a little flour each time if the sheet is sticky.
7. Continue setting the rollers to the next narrower setting and pass the dough through, always starting at an open end. Cut the sheet in half for easier handling. Continue narrowing the settings to stretch the dough to about 1/16-inch.

It should be pretty obvious as you read these instructions that:

1. The flour wall surrounding the well is a pretty fragile affair.
2. The dried globules of dough will make holes in the delicate finished product. My first and second attempts resembled alligator skin.
3. Stretching the dough by hand through 8 consecutive roller settings put me on a direct route to carpal tunnel syndrome. Fortunately, I discovered the existence of a pasta motor. It attaches to most hand-cranked pasta machines. It was invented, no doubt, by a person who needs two hands to do everything in life.

Even though it is a challenging culinary exercise, making fresh pasta can only embolden the home chef to make ravioli, filled cannelloni, and tortellini. No filled pasta is possible without homemade fresh pasta.

Food Processor Dough—The Alternative *(Ravioli)*

My cousin, John Rissetto, was an aspiring chef in his high school days. But his desire to unearth clues to our civilization put cheffing on the back burner. John is now defending his dissertation outline toward a PhD in archaeology. When he returns to Falls Church from his worldwide digs at Christmastime, he makes dough for 300 ravioli for Christmas dinner. Here is his perfected recipe for pasta dough made in a food processor.

One dough ball will make approximately 36 ravioli using a standard ravioli mold.

2 c. flour
2 eggs
1/4 tsp. salt
2 Tbsp. olive oil
5 to 7 Tbsp. warm water

Procedure for forming ravioli:

1. Line 2 large baking sheets with clean kitchen towels.
2. Place flour and salt in the mixing bowl of the food processor. Pulse 5 seconds.
3. In a small bowl, using a fork, combine eggs and olive oil. With the processor running, add the mixture to the flour and process 5 seconds.
4. With the processor running, add the warm water, 1 tablespoon at a time until the ingredients form a ball.
5. Remove the dough from the processor and place on a board. Knead a little flour into the dough by hand. Knead for 2–3 minutes so it's easier to handle. Divide the dough in half and wrap in plastic. Place in a warm, dry place for approximately 1 hour to allow the gluten to relax.
6. Working with 1 piece at a time, form the dough into a rectangle. Set the pasta machine at #1, the widest setting. Pass the dough through, then trifold the extruded dough into a package, as you would a letter. Place an open end of the folded dough through the machine on the same setting. Repeat this process about 6 times, dusting with a little flour each time if the sheet is sticky.

7. Continue setting the rollers to the next narrower setting and pass the dough through, always starting at an open end. Cut the sheet in half for easier handling. Continue narrowing the settings to stretch the dough to about 1/16-inch.
8. Drop the filling by ample teaspoonfuls at 1-inch intervals along one side of the dough. Fold the dough over the filling to the opposite edge. Using your fingers, press the pasta down between the mounds and along the edges to seal it.
9. Cut between the mounds to form squares using a ravioli cutter.
10. Place the ravioli on baking sheets on the kitchen towels that have been sprinkled with cornmeal.
11. Repeat the procedure until all the filling is used. Cook or freeze.
12. Cook the ravioli 8 or 10 at a time in ample amounts of boiling salted water. Remove with a slotted spoon.

To freeze:
Dry the ravioli on clean cloths in a cool room. Dust liberally with corn meal, turn three times between 12 and 24 hours. Store in plastic bags up to 2 months.

To cut pasta for spaghetti, fettuccine, or linguine:
Go to the next to the last setting on the pasta machine. Bundle the pasta and allow to dry completely on kitchen towels before storing in plastic containers.

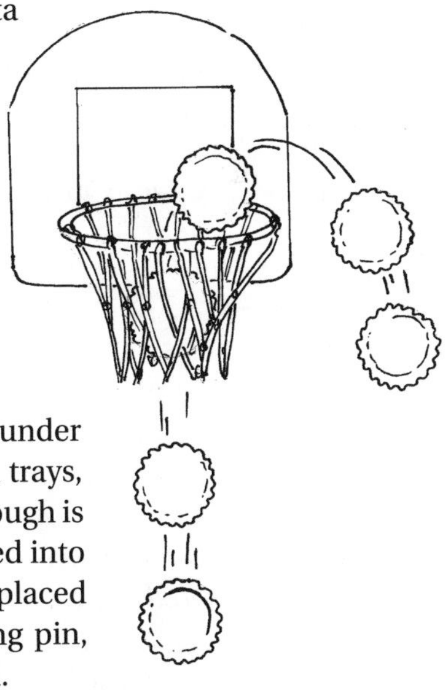

Ravioli:

Stretch to the last setting. Form the ravioli without drying the strips. The slightly supple dough will easily adhere to itself.

Note: Kitchen shops stock ravioli forms under various brand names. They are small metal trays, with depressions for fillings. One sheet of dough is laid over the tray and the fillings are dropped into the depressions. Another sheet of dough is placed on top and then rolled firmly with a rolling pin, which then seals and cuts individual ravioli.

The Best Amateur Chef in D.C

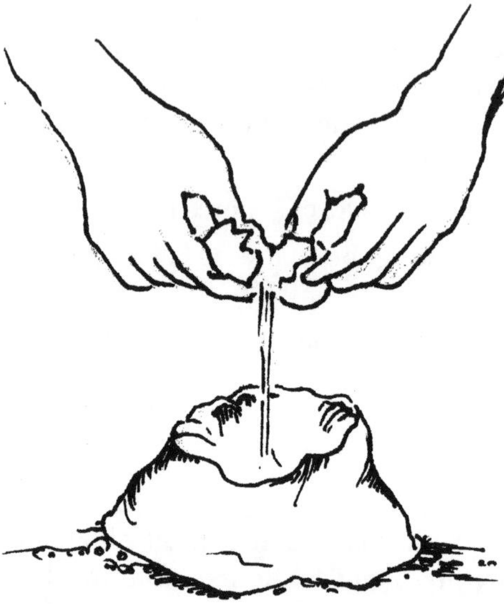

My son, Bob Gambarelli, created this award-winning recipe. Bob is the Guidance Director at James Madison High School in Vienna, and he won an amateur cooking contest sponsored by Il Maggiano's, a restaurant in Tyson's Corner, Virginia. Bob was dubbed "Washington's Best Italian Cook" and was rewarded with two plane tickets to Italy, a week's stay at deluxe hotels in the Tuscany region, and private tours of wineries, including tasting and lunches, plus $1000. Bob's dish was included on the October menu at Maggiano's. He was particularly gratified that for every order, a portion of the proceeds was donated to the Ronald McDonald House.

Bob made many trial runs with his wife, Peggy, when they fiddled with the filling. The first time he experimented with the dish, he didn't know that duck breasts existed. "I actually bought three ducks and hung them from the basement ceiling to bleed. When I went down and saw the ducks hanging from the laundry pipes, I wondered, what am I doing here?"

Bob says that making ravioli is a two-person operation and is fun to do when you have guests. "Everyone has a glass of wine and the ravioli turn out great." He says he has a healthy respect for professional chefs and doesn't plan to quit his day job.

Ravioli with a Duck and Spinach Filling in a Porcini Cream Sauce

Follow directions for Food Processor Method or Homemade Fresh Pasta to make the ravioli.

WINE SUGGESTION: Burgundy or Pinot Grigio

Duck Filling:

1 lb. fresh spinach, stems trimmed, washed. Boil 2–3 minutes. Drain. Squeeze dry and chop. Set aside.
4 Tbsp. olive oil
1 bay leaf
1 clove garlic, minced
12 oz. duck breast, coarsely chopped
3 large eggs, beaten with a fork
1 lb. ricotta
4 Tbsp. Parmesan cheese, freshly grated
freshly grated nutmeg, to taste
salt and freshly ground pepper to taste

1. In a large skillet, heat 2 tablespoons olive oil. Add bay leaf and garlic and sauté 1 minute.
2. Add remaining oil, duck, salt, and pepper and sauté 5 minutes. Discard the bay leaf. Cool.
3. Transfer the mixture to a large bowl. Add the eggs, ricotta, and Parmesan cheese. Mix well to combine. Add nutmeg and correct for seasonings.

Porcini Cream Sauce:

1 oz. dried porcini mushrooms, steeped in 1 cup hot water for 30 minutes. Strain and reserve liquid.
2 Tbsp. olive oil
1 shallot, minced
1 c. heavy cream
2/3 c. Parmesan cheese, freshly grated

salt and freshly ground pepper to taste
freshly ground nutmeg to taste
reserved mushroom liquid

1. Squeeze the liquid from the mushrooms and remove them to a cutting board and coarsely chop.
2. In a saucepan, sauté the shallot, over medium heat, in the oil until soft and translucent, about 3 minutes.
3. Add the mushrooms, salt, and pepper. Cook about 3 minutes. Add the cream, cheese, salt and pepper, and nutmeg. Cook about 2 minutes. Add the porcini liquid, with stirring.
4. Cook over low heat until the sauce has been reduced to the consistency of heavy cream, about 20–25 minutes, stirring frequently.

Presentation:

Cook the homemade ravioli in salted boiling water until the pasta is cooked. Timing will depend on the thickness of the pasta dough. Drain in a colander or remove with a slotted spoon and transfer to a large bowl. Gently toss the ravioli with the porcini cream sauce and serve immediately.

My Mother's Genoese Ravioli Filling

(Enough for approximately 150 ravioli)

My daughter Nina declares that her grandmother's ravioli filling is "the best." Since Nina and my mother, Catherine, are "surrealistically" connected, it must be true. Nina says learning to make fresh pasta put her on a fast track to ravioli making. Always available in her freezer, they are the stars in many of her gourmet dinners.

Follow directions for Food Processor Method or Homemade Fresh Pasta to make ravioli dough.

Meat filling:

The filling may be made and refrigerated 1 day ahead.

12 oz. chicken or turkey breast, poached (cooked in *simmering,* not boiling, water) and chopped very fine or ground in a food processor

4 oz. ground veal or sirloin

1 pkg. frozen chopped spinach, cooked according to the package instructions and pressed to remove the liquid

1 small onion finely chopped

2 Tbsp. olive oil

1 Tbsp. unsalted butter

2 eggs, beaten in a small bowl with a fork

15 oz. whole milk ricotta, drained to remove liquid

1 c. Parmesan cheese, freshly grated

2 Tbsp. unflavored breadcrumbs

1/8 tsp. ground nutmeg

salt and freshly ground pepper to taste

1. Poach the chicken breast in a covered saucepan for 20 minutes or until done. Cool.
2. Process the chicken in a food processor.
3. Cook the spinach as directed on the package. Drain, press out the liquid, and process in the food processor until fine.

4. In a large skillet, heat the oil and butter. Add the onion and cook, over moderate heat, until translucent, about 10 minutes.
5. Add the veal or sirloin and cook briefly. Drain off the excess fat.
6. To a large bowl, add the processed chicken, meat, spinach, eggs, ricotta, Parmesan cheese, bread crumbs, nutmeg, and salt and pepper.
7. Mix well, cover with plastic wrap and refrigerate until ready to form the ravioli.

Crespelle: Pasta's Alter Ego

Making crespelle or crepes is a no-fail way to create delicious cannelloni. Crespelle are made from a thin pancake batter and replace the usual fresh or dried pasta in the preparation of cannelloni or manicotti. They can be filled with a variety of cooked stuffings, meat, cheese, or vegetables, or a combination of all three and made ahead in stages.

- Make the sauce and refrigerate up to 2 days ahead, or freeze.
- Make the filling and store in the refrigerator up to 1 day ahead.
- Make the crepes. They can be made a few days ahead. Refrigerate or freeze.
- The completed dish can be assembled and held, refrigerated, up to 1 day ahead or frozen up to 1 month before popping it in the oven.

Cannelloni Filled with Three Cheeses

(Yield: approximately 16 crepes)

Crespelle alla fiorentina is a famous Florentine dish featuring crepes stuffed with spinach, ricotta, and Parmesan cheese, topped with béchamel and tomato sauce, and baked.

Make the crepes in a blender or by hand using a whisk. In either case, refrigerate the mixture for an hour to dispel the air bubbles. The crepes can be made in advance, stacked individually with wax paper, then refrigerated or frozen until ready to use.

WINE SUGGESTION: Pinot Bianco

Crepes:

1 c. milk
1 c. all purpose flour
pinch of salt
2 eggs, beaten with a fork
1 Tbsp. butter, melted and cooled
2 Tbsp. butter, melted, to brush the pan

1. Pour the milk into a medium-size bowl. Using a whisk or blender, slowly add the flour and salt until thoroughly blended. Stir in the beaten eggs and the cooled melted butter. Refrigerate the batter for 1 hour to dispel the air bubbles.
2. Using a 7- or 8-inch non-stick skillet or crepe pan, heat the pan over moderate heat, then brush the pan with melted butter.
3. Spoon 2 tablespoons batter into the center of the pan. Lift the pan from the heat and rotate so that the batter completely covers the surface of the pan. The crepe will form very quickly. Return the pan to the heat and cook until the crepe is a deep yellow color, about 1 minute. Using a spatula, flip the pancake and briefly cook on the other side.
4. Transfer the crepes to a plate, layering each crepe with wax paper. Continue cooking, taking care to keep them from becoming crisp. If a non-stick or crepe pan is used, it need not be buttered each time.

Filling:

1 10-oz. package frozen chopped spinach, cooked according to the package directions. Drain. When cool, squeeze dry and chop fine.

1 15-oz. container whole milk ricotta

1 egg +1 egg yolk

1/2 c. Parmesan cheese, freshly grated

salt to taste

1/4 c. Italian Fontina, grated

freshly ground pepper

freshly ground nutmeg or 1/8th teaspoon of ground nutmeg

Put all the ingredients in a large bowl and mix well. Cover and set aside.

Béchamel Sauce (Yield: 1 2/3 cups)

2 c. milk

4 Tbsp. unsalted butter

3 Tbsp. flour

1/4 tsp. salt

pinch nutmeg

freshly ground pepper to taste

1. Warm the milk in a saucepan.
2. In another saucepan, melt the butter over moderately low heat.
3. Add the flour to the melted butter, stirring constantly with a wooden spoon. Cook over low heat, 3–5 minutes.
4. Add the hot milk all at once and stir constantly until it thickens.
5. Add the salt, nutmeg, and pepper.
6. Cover with plastic wrap. Set aside.

Tomato Sauce

2 Tbsp. olive oil

1 small onion, minced

1 carrot, chopped fine

1 rib celery, chopped fine
2 Tbsp. minced Italian flat-leaf parsley
2 or 3 basil leaves (optional)
1/4 c. dry white wine or dry vermouth
1 28-oz. can good quality plum tomatoes, chopped, or passed through a food mill

1. In a medium saucepan, heat the oil over moderate heat.
2. Add the onion, carrot, and celery. Stir and cook until the vegetables soften, about 10 minutes.
3. Add the parsley, basil, and the wine or vermouth. Cook until the alcohol dissipates, about 2 minutes.
4. Add the tomatoes; cook uncovered, over low to moderate heat, about 20–25 minutes.

The cooked sauce can be passed through a food mill or processed in a food processor to achieve a creamier consistency. It's your call.

Assembly:

Adjust the oven rack to the top level. Preheat the oven to 400 degrees.

1. Butter the bottom and sides of a 9x12-inch oven-proof baking pan. The number of required pans depends on how many cannelloni you are making. Spoon 3 tablespoons of tomato sauce on the bottom of the pans.
2. Lay a crespella on a work surface. Spoon about 2 tablespoons of the filling down the center of the crepe, leaving a 1/2-inch border on all sides. Fold over one side to cover the filling, then bring the other side to the opposite edge. Place the cannelloni in the pan but do not crowd them. The eggs in the batter will puff up the crepes. Give them room to expand. Repeat the process until all the crepes are filled.
3. Arrange the filled crepes in a single layer in the pan.
4. Lightly spoon tomato sauce on each cannelloni, covering all the edges.
5. Spoon some béchamel on the tomato sauce.
6. Bake the cannelloni, uncovered, for 15 minutes. If they have been refrigerated or frozen, bring to room temperature before baking.
7. Let the cannelloni rest 5 minutes. Sprinkle a teaspoon or two of Parmesan cheese on each cannelloni before serving.

Gnocchi: Potato Dumplings

I grew up in an Italian enclave in Greenwich Village where spirited discussions invariably centered on the merits of the three New York baseball teams, the Giants, Yankees, and Brooklyn Dodgers—and food! In those days, families and extended families lived in close proximity to each other, so it was not unusual for vigorous baseball imbroglios to take place daily on the sidewalks of New York.

Uncle Tony preserved the food traditions of our family in my grandfather's groceria. When the Prohibition Amendment was repealed, my Uncle Harry decided to open a liquor store next to Uncle Tony's grocery store. Uncle Harry graduated from Georgetown University's Law School but bypassed a legal career at the height of the Depression. The brothers worked in tandem, but they were on opposite sides of the baseball fence. Not a day passed that my two uncles didn't argue the fortunes of the ignominious Giants, versus the latest acquisition of the affluent Yankee organization.

But it wasn't all about baseball. How could it be, with the aroma of prosciutto in the air and an outstanding bottle of red wine ready to be uncorked? I was oblivious then, to the cuisine of my heritage and far more interested in extolling the virtues of the Giants versus the enemy, the Brooklyn Dodgers. It was not until many years later that I, in the throes of my new cooking career, had more than a spirited discussion with my Uncle Harry as we compared the quality of a gnocco made with or without an egg. We were having dinner together in a popular Greenwich Village trattoria when I took the plunge and ordered a dish of gnocchi di patate (potato gnocchi). Given the restaurant's reputation, they should have been as light as a feather. To my dismay, after the first bite, I could only stare sadly at that plateful of lead balloons. I immediately concluded that an egg had made its way into the chef's gnocchi recipe. That's when the culinary fight began. Uncle Harry insisted that for ease of preparation, an egg must be included in the recipe. I, who wished for a lighter and less dense gnocco, chose to forever banish the egg from my potato gnocchi. We were on opposite sides of the culinary fence. Certainly, the addition of an egg to the dough makes it a little easier to handle but a few tries without an egg transforms the gnocchi novice into the egg-less pro. Uncle Harry didn't seem to trust my new-found knowledge. It was a baseball battle all over again. Nobody gave in.

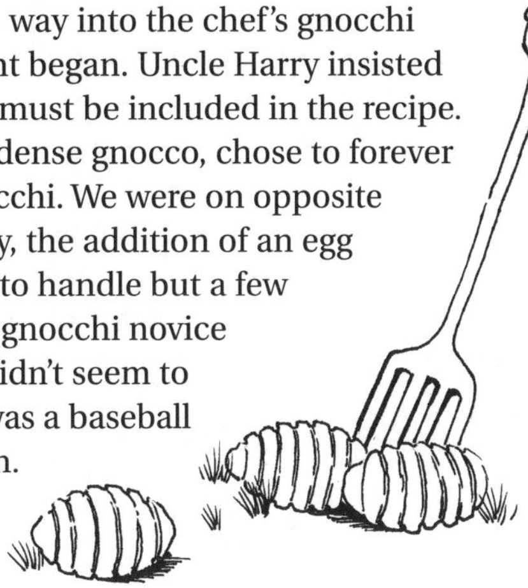

Potato Gnocchi

(About 6 servings as a 1st course)

Gnocchi marry well with a myriad of sauces: Pesto, Bolognese, Tomato Porcini, or a Fresh Tomato sauce to name just a few. The grooves made by the tines of the fork will hold the sauce. It only takes about 15–20 minutes to form potato gnocchi and cook them on the spot. Just have the sauce ready!

2 lbs. Idaho or Russet potatoes
About 1 1/4 c. all purpose flour, plus more if needed
2 tsp. salt

Procedure:

1. Boil the potatoes in their jackets until tender, about 20–25 minutes, depending on the size of the potato. Lightly flour a baking sheet. Set aside.
2. Place the flour and salt on a work surface. When the potatoes are cooked and just cool enough to handle, remove the skin, and pass them through a ricer or food mill directly into the flour while still warm.
3. Knead the mixture with your fingers until it holds together. Potatoes vary in their moisture content, so the proportion of potato to flour may vary.
4. Turn the dough out onto a lightly floured surface and knead gently with lightly floured hands until the dough is smooth. Work in more flour if the dough is too sticky.
5. Divide the dough into 8 pieces. Take 1 piece and cover rest of the dough with a clean cloth.
6. Roll the dough into a long rope about 1-inch in diameter. Cut the rope into 1/2-inch pieces
7. Hold a fork above the work surface with the concave part facing up and the tip of the fork facing away from you. Using your thumb, gently roll 1 piece of the dough against the inside tines of the fork and toward the tip onto the floured baking sheet. It will form a dumpling with ridges on one side and a deep indentation from the tines on the other. Continue the procedure until all the dough is used.

To cook the gnocchi:

1. Bring a large pot of water to a boil and add salt.
2. Cook in two batches. Drop half the gnocchi into the boiling water.
3. Cook, stirring gently, for about 1 minute or until they rise to the surface.
4. Remove the gnocchi with a large slotted spoon or skimmer to a platter or low bowl and dress with the sauce of your choice.
5. Cook the remaining gnocchi and add more sauce.

Gnocchi Verdi

(Serves 6–8)

In Italy, gnocchi verdi (green dumplings) are sometimes playfully called ravioli in camicia (ravioli in their undershirts) or ravioli nudi because they are merely filling with no pasta covering. They are shaped like dumplings, then poached and gratineed.

WINE SUGGESTION: Pinot Grigio

Preheat oven to 375 degrees

- 1 small onion, minced
- 2 Tbsp. unsalted butter
- 1 10-oz. pkg. frozen chopped spinach. Cook according to the package directions, drain, **squeeze dry** and chop fine. Cool.
- 15 oz. ricotta
- 2 large eggs, slightly beaten
- 3/4 c. Parmigiano Reggiano, freshly grated. Reserve 1/4 cup.
- a few grindings of fresh nutmeg
- 1/4 lb. (1 stick) unsalted butter, melted
- 6 Tbsp. flour
- 5 or 6 twists of the peppermill
- salt to taste

1. In a small skillet over medium heat, sauté the onion in the butter until the onion is soft.
2. Transfer the spinach to a large bowl. Add the ricotta, eggs, 1/2 cup Parmesan cheese, onion, nutmeg, 4 tablespoons flour, pepper, and salt to taste. Mix well and refrigerate for at least 1 hour. *The recipe can be held and refrigerated at this point.*
3. Bring 6 cups water to a boil. Shape a couple of gnocchi into walnut-size balls and roll in some flour. Carefully drop them into the water and poach for 2–3 minutes or just until they rise to the top. If the gnocchi hold their shape, finish forming the rest. Roll them in flour and poach them a few at a time. If the mixture is too soft, add 2 tablespoons flour to stiffen.

4. Gently lift the gnocchi out of the water with a slotted spoon and arrange them in a single layer in an oven proof dish or large gratin pan which has been coated with half the melted butter. When all the dumplings have been added to the pan, drizzle with the remaining butter and sprinkle with the reserved Parmesan cheese.
5. Bake for 10 minutes or until the cheese is lightly browned.

Ricotta Gnocchi in Pink Vodka Sauce

(Serves 6–8)

These little upstarts look just like their parents, potato gnocchi, but we've taken a shortcut in the preparation. Instead of boiling and peeling potatoes, ricotta and Parmesan cheese are the magic ingredients. And when it's all over, these ricotta dumplings can go directly into a pot of boiling water or to the freezer. Add a splash of Vodka and you have a delectable dish.

WINE SUGGESTION: Chianti Classico

1 15-oz. container whole milk ricotta, drained
1 1/4 c. Parmesan cheese, freshly grated, about 5 oz. Reserve 1/4 cup
1/2 tsp. salt
approximately 2 c. all purpose flour

1. In a large bowl, mix the ricotta with 1 cup of the Parmesan cheese until well blended.
2. Gradually stir in as much flour as possible with a wooden spoon.
3. When the dough becomes too stiff to stir, turn it out onto a floured board. Knead in the remaining flour until it is smooth, is not sticky, and it forms a ball.
4. Cut off 1/8th of the dough and cover the remaining portion with a clean cloth.
5. Roll the cut piece of dough into a cylinder, about 3/4-inch in diameter. With a sharp knife, cut the cylinder into 3/4-inch lengths.
6. Holding a fork in one hand and using the thumb of the other hand, roll each dumpling off the inside tines of a fork on the side that is not cut. Use just enough pressure to make ridges on one side and a concave depression on the other. Flour the fork if the gnocchi stick to the tines.
7. Put the gnocchi on a clean kitchen cloth in a cool place. Repeat the procedure with the remaining dough, adding small amounts of flour if the dough becomes too sticky to handle.
8. Cook the gnocchi in batches in salted, boiling water until they rise to the top. Remove with a slotted spoon to a large bowl and dress lightly with the vodka sauce.
9. Top the individual servings with the reserved cheese.

To freeze:

Arrange the gnocchi in a single layer on a cookie sheet. Freeze until firm then transfer to plastic containers. They may be cooked frozen but allow 2–3 minutes more of cooking time.

Pink Vodka Sauce:

6 Tbsp. unsalted butter
1/2 c. vodka
1 c. heavy cream
2 8-oz. cans tomato sauce
1/2 tsp. salt

1. In a skillet or sauté pan, melt the butter over moderate heat.
2. Add the vodka and simmer about 2 minutes.
3. Add the cream and tomato sauce. Simmer, uncovered, 5–7 minutes.

Gnocchi alla Romana

Gnocchi in the Roman style, Semolina cakes baked with butter and cheese

(Serves 6)

These gnocchi are small tender dumplings made with semolina flour, eggs, milk, and cheese. The exact proportion of semolina to milk depends on the fineness of the semolina grind. If the semolina is very fine, then more is needed. These gnocchi are more easily formed if the mixture is allowed to set overnight. Semolina should be bought in small quantities and stored in a dry place.

WINE SUGGESTION: Verdicchio

Preheat oven to 350 degrees

1 qt. whole milk
3 Tbsp. unsalted butter
pinch salt
pinch nutmeg
approximately 3 1/2 cups semolina
3 egg yolks
1/3 c. Parmesan cheese

Sauce:

4 Tbsp. unsalted butter, melted
2/3 c. Parmesan cheese, freshly grated

1. In a large saucepan, combine the milk, butter, salt, and nutmeg and heat to boiling.
2. Gradually add the semolina in a steady stream, stirring constantly with a wooden spoon. Continue cooking and stirring until the mixture becomes as thick as oatmeal and starts to pull away from the bottom and sides of the pan.
3. Remove the pot from the heat. Add the yolks, while stirring, one at a time. Add the cheese.

4. Pour the mixture on to a flat, buttered baking sheet and spread to 1/2-inch layer.
5. Cover with plastic wrap and refrigerate until cool, or overnight.
6. Using a 2-inch cookie cutter, cut the mixture into discs. Transfer the discs to a 12x9-inch buttered baking dish, overlapping them slightly.
7. Drizzle with 4 tablespoons melted butter.
8. Bake 15–20 minutes.
9. Sprinkle with Parmesan cheese before serving.

Gnocchi with Butter and Sage

(Serves 4–6 as a first course)

Gnocchi easily adapt to a wide variety of sauces. The choices seem endless. They run the gamut from tomato, meat, cheese, and cream. Pairing fresh sage leaves and butter with the gnocchi in this recipe gives these delectable dumplings a delicious spin.

1 Recipe Potato Gnocchi cooked as directed.

Sage/Butter Sauce:

3 Tbsp. unsalted butter
12 fresh sage leaves
salt and freshly ground pepper to taste
Parmesan cheese, freshly grated

1. In a large 12-inch skillet or chef's pan, preferably non-stick, over medium-low heat, melt the butter with the sage.
2. Add the cooked gnocchi to the pan and reduce the heat to low.
3. Cook, stirring gently, until they are warmed through.
4. Add the salt and freshly ground pepper.
5. Sprinkle individual portions with Parmesan cheese.

Time for a Spaghettata
a.k.a. Spaghetti Orgy

Years ago, as we left the James Beard House after a meeting, a colleague suggested we go to her apartment in Greenwich Village for a "spaghettata." I had no idea what was in store, but Rudy and I were delighted to be invited because her distinguished reputation as a cook was well known.

She poured us a glass of wine, put water in a couple of pots, and made two sauces in no time flat. She dressed penne and fettuccine with the sauces, passed the freshly grated cheese, and poured more wine. Hazelnut biscotti and espresso finished up the meal. I couldn't help thinking that the spontaneity of the invitation and the delightful informality of the dinner so aptly demonstrated the friendly qualities so dominant in the Italian personality.

Months later, I spied a large ceramic dish in a kitchen shop which was a perfect bowl from which to serve pasta. The word "Spaghettata" leapt out at me, along with the sauce recipe written in Italian. I've been intrigued with the word and its possibilities ever since, so here goes.

It's time to have some fun with the recipes in this book. You may have guessed from the title of this chapter that a spaghettata will be a test of your ability to host an incomparable party with pasta as the star.

Game Plan

1. Decide on the number of guests. Eight is a workable number. Everyone, then, has the opportunity to work or observe the pasta-making process.
2. Pick a date and time. Send out the invitations. Ask your friends to bring a bottle of wine.
3. Decide on a theme: Think Italian. Choose the colors (red, white, and green are an obvious choice); flowers (such as sunflowers) for the table centerpiece; napkins, nametags, and place cards. Supply aprons for all.
4. Select the menu and print a complete set of recipes for each participant.
5. Set the table whenever it's convenient during the week of the party. Have enough plates for each pasta dish. Have wine glasses sparkling clean and ready to go.

6. If you have chosen recipes that can be prepared ahead, do it when convenient.
7. Make the dessert and bread the day before the party, or buy hearty Italian bread.
8. Prepare the Antipasto.
9. If possible, set up four workstations in the kitchen. Two guests per team can work together on a recipe.
10. The morning of the orgy, arrange plates on a serving space. The pasta will be plated there.
11. Assign the teams when the guests arrive. Review the recipes. Answer questions.

Suggested Menu

The guests can sample the antipasto and critique the wine while the orgy is in progress.

1. *Antipasto Platter:* a selection of cured meats such as prosciutto, salami, mortadella; patés; pickles, olives, pepperoncini, roasted red peppers, bean salad; a selection of Italian cheeses such as Parmigiano-Reggiano, Pecorino Romano, Fontina; breadsticks, sausage bread, bruschetta, focaccia, and a hearty loaf of Tuscan bread. Recipe follows.
2. *Cannelloni Filled with Three Cheeses:* (Recipe appears earlier in this section.) Team 1 makes the crêpes. The filling and sauces have been made ahead. The dish is assembled and baked by the team.
3. *Fettuccine with a Pesto Sauce:* See pasta method at the beginning of this section and the pesto sauce recipe in the "Eat Your Veggies" section. The pesto sauce has been made ahead. Teams 2 and 3 make the pasta as directed, by hand or in the food processor. Teams 1 and 4 should take turns stretching and cutting the dough.
4. *Ricotta Gnocchi in a Pink Vodka Sauce:* (Recipe appears earlier in this section.) Team 4 makes the gnocchi. Call for more volunteers here. Team 2 makes the Vodka Sauce.
5. *Amaretto Mousse:* Recipe follows.

Enjoy!

Homemade Bread: Nothing Tastes Better Than This

Let's take the worry and the mystery out of that little 1/4-oz. package of active dry yeast. So many homemade bread lovers are fearful that they will kill off the yeast in the bread making process, so the recipe languishes in the recipe box never to be tried. Here are some tips to take you on the road to romance singing, "A Jug of Wine, a Loaf of Bread and Thou."

A **thermometer** is an invaluable tool in bread making. If liquids are too hot, the yeast will be killed; if too cool, the yeast will not dissolve. The yeast mystique is easily dispelled with a thermometer. Buy a yogurt/yeast thermometer with fewer increments than a candy thermometer. It will read 32–220 degrees and is available at all hardware stores.

Yeast is the leavening agent for bread. It makes the dough rise and the bread light. Compressed yeast and active dry yeast can be used interchangeably. 1 pkg. of dry yeast equals one 0.6 oz. cake. The Conventional method (yeast dissolved in water at 105–115 degrees) or the Rapid Rise Method (the liquid is added to the yeast in combination with the dry ingredients at 120–130 degrees) are both acceptable. Store the compressed yeast on a cool, dry shelf and keep an eye on the expiration date.

Flour: Always use unbleached, unsifted, all purpose flour. All purpose flour is milled from a combination of high-gluten hard wheat and lower-gluten soft wheat. Bread flour, now available in supermarkets, contains a higher percentage of gluten and is milled solely from hard wheat. The gluten protein stretches the elastic network that traps the gas bubbles formed by the yeast and structures the loaf. Flours with the highest gluten content produce breads with the biggest volume.

Kneading: Strong kneading makes the gluten develop faster. Fold the dough toward you and push away with the heel of your hand while turning the dough 1/4 turn. You can also use an electric mixer equipped with a dough hook or a food processor that can handle 5 cups of flour.

Rising: An even temperature of 80–85 degrees, free of drafts, is ideal. You can achieve this environment by setting the bowl of dough in an unlit oven over a pan of hot water.

Baking: Bake in a preheated, 450-degree oven.

Cooling: Immediately remove the bread from cloche (an instant brick oven) and place on a wire rack to cool.

Rudy's Tuscan Bread

Rudy bought a Cloche from Williams-Sonoma a few years ago and it's been non-stop bread making ever since. The domed top or cover, is a half-sphere which fits into a shallow round of unglazed stoneware simulating "an oven within an oven." The resulting bread is golden brown and crusty.

Use an electric mixer equipped with a dough hook or a food processor that can handle 5 cups of flour. Strictly speaking, true Tuscan bread is saltless because it is used as a base for salted soups and sauces. Rudy puts in the salt and he calls it Tuscan bread, anyway.

1 pkg. Fleischmann's Rapid Rise yeast
1 tsp. sugar
1 Tbsp. salt
5 c. unbleached, all purpose flour
1 3/4 c. water (120–130 degrees)

1. Combine the yeast, sugar, salt, and flour in the bowl of an electric mixer. Attach the dough hook.
2. With the machine running, gradually add the hot water. Mix thoroughly. Knead the dough about 5 minutes by machine, or 8–10 minutes by hand or until the dough is smooth as a baby's bottom and elastic.

3. Transfer the dough to a large bowl, cover with plastic wrap AND a clean kitchen cloth and place in a warm, draft-free environment until doubled in bulk (about 1 hour).
4. Punch the dough down, place on a floured board and knead for 2–3 minutes. Let rest, covered with the cloth, for 5 minutes.
5. Sprinkle the bottom of the cloche with cornmeal.
6. Form the dough into a ball and transfer to the cloche.
7. Cover and let rise in a warm place free from drafts until doubled in bulk, about 1 hour.
8. Preheat oven to 450 degrees. Slash the top of the dough with a sharp knife, cover and place the pan in the middle of the oven. Bake 15 minutes.
9. Reduce heat to 400 degrees and continue baking for 35–40 minutes or until the bread is crusty and golden brown. Remove the cover after 35 minutes and bake 5 minutes longer.
10. Remove the bread and transfer to a wire rack to cool.

Amaretto Mousse

(Serves 8–10)

Bask in the afterglow of a great meal. Indulge in a delectable dessert infused with a hint of amaretto.

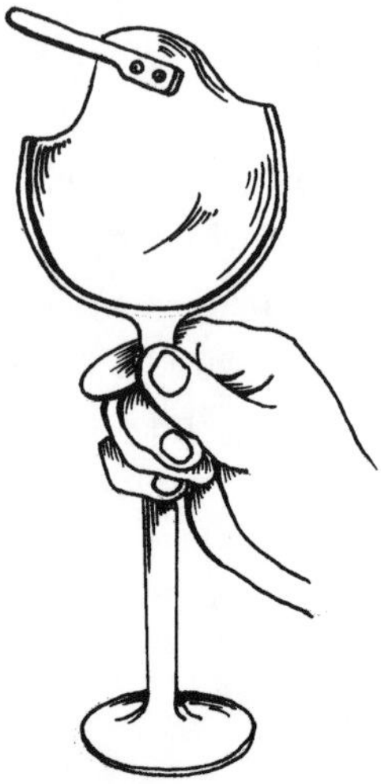

5 large eggs, separated
1/2 c. sugar
pinch salt
1 tsp. vanilla extract
1 c. whole milk
1 envelope Knox unflavored gelatin
3 Tbsp. cold water
1 pt. heavy whipping cream
3 oz. Amaretto Liqueur
3 Amaretto cookies, crushed, optional
additional Amaretto, optional

1. In a medium-sized bowl, using a whisk, beat the egg yolks with the sugar until light yellow in color. Transfer the mixture to a medium saucepan.
2. In another saucepan, bring the milk to a boil. Add the vanilla.
3. Slowly add the milk to the egg yolk mixture and stir thoroughly. Cook over low heat, stirring constantly. Do not allow the mixture to boil. Remove from the heat and transfer to a bowl. Set aside.
4. Put 3 tablespoons cold water in a small Pyrex custard cup. Add the gelatin. Place the cup in a small saucepan of hot water to dissolve and soften the gelatin.
5. Add the dissolved gelatin to the egg yolk/milk mixture and place the bowl in an ice bath to hasten the cooling. Add the Amaretto.
6. Beat the cream until stiff. In another bowl, beat the egg whites with the salt until they form soft peaks.
7. Using a spatula or large whisk, fold the beaten cream into the mixture. Fold in the egg whites.
8. Select 10 champagne flutes, stemmed glasses, or wine goblets. Divide the crumbled Amaretto cookies in the bottom of the glasses. Add 1 teaspoon Amaretto. Spoon the mousse into the glasses and sprinkle a few crumbs over the mousse. Refrigerate 6 hours or overnight.

The Fun Is Done...It's Time To Party!

Section V

Beyond Pasta

The recipes in this section will round out your repertoire and take your cooking skills beyond pasta. Choose an appetizer, main course, bread, and a delectable dessert for a special dinner party.

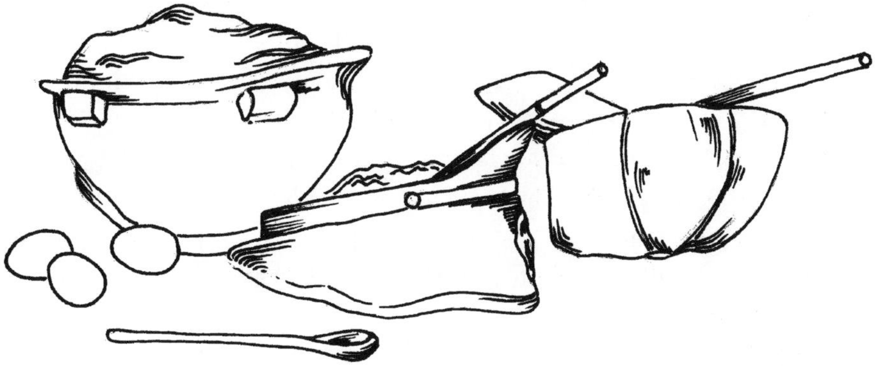

My Mother's Minestrone, Genoa Style
(A hearty vegetable soup)

Minestrone appeared on my mother, Catherine's, table most often during snowy New York winters. Her secret ingredient: Parmigiano rinds, which she stashed in the freezer for moments like this.

1/2 c. Ditalini, small tubular pasta
1/4 c. olive oil
1 medium onion, diced
3 leeks, white only, rinsed and sliced fine
3 carrots, scrubbed clean, peeled and diced
2 ribs celery, diced
2 small potatoes, diced
2 medium zucchini, diced
a prosciutto bone (if you're lucky), or a ham bone or 3 oz. salt pork. Alternatively, 3 oz. prosciutto or ham in one piece
1 qt. chicken stock, canned or homemade
2 qts. water
1/2 lb. fresh peas or 1 pkg. frozen
1 16-oz. can diced tomatoes or 1 cup fresh plum tomatoes, diced
2/3 c. Great Northern beans soaked in water for a few hours, or overnight. Substitute fresh cranberry beans, if available at the market.
1 bay leaf
3 Tbsp. minced fresh basil
salt and freshly ground pepper
Parmigiano Reggiano, freshly grated

1. In a large stockpot, warm the oil.
2. Add the onion and leeks. Sauté until the vegetables are soft.
3. Stir in the carrots, celery, potatoes, and zucchini. Cook briefly, with stirring.
4. Add the prosciutto, salt pork, or ham bone, the stock, water, peas, toma-

toes, beans, bay leaf, basil, salt, and freshly ground pepper.

5. Cover and simmer over low heat for about 2 hours.
6. Add the ditalini and cook to *al dente. Minestrone is a thick soup, but sometimes the pasta soaks up all the broth. Add more chicken stock, if necessary. Use low-salt canned chicken soup.*

Minestrone keeps well in the refrigerator for up to one week.

Caviar Eclipse

This elegant but simple hors d'oeuvre makes a striking presentation. Black Lumpfish masquerading as Caviar is guaranteed to impress your guests.

6 hard boiled eggs, finely chopped
1 medium red onion, finely chopped
6 Tbsp. unsalted butter, melted
freshly ground pepper, to taste
1 c. sour cream, total
2 3 1/2-oz. black lumpfish caviar
Melba toast

Garnish:

2 oz. softened cream cheese combined with 1/4 cup sour cream

1. In a bowl, combine the eggs, onion, butter, and 1/4 cup sour cream.
2. Spread the mixture into an 8-inch glass pie plate.
3. Spread 1/2 cup sour cream over the egg mixture, cover with plastic wrap and refrigerate for at least 4 hours, or overnight.
4. Put the caviar in a fine mesh sieve. Rinse with cold water to get rid of the black liquid. Spread the caviar onto paper towels to dry briefly. This step prevents the black color of the lumpfish from bleeding into the sour cream.
5. Scoop up the caviar and spread it evenly over the sour cream.
6. In a small bowl, combine remaining sour cream and cream cheese and blend until smooth.
7. Garnish with small dollops of the mixture on the outer rim.
8. Set the plate on a larger plate and fan Melba toast or endive leaves between the plates.

Pepperoni Batter Bread

(Yield: 1 round loaf)

Pepperoni and a ***no-knead*** *easy preparation puts this bread high on my list. It's a spunky addition to any meal. The batter is mixed and allowed to rise in the pan and then baked. No need to knead.*

Preheat oven to 350 degrees

Butter a 1 1/2-qt. oven-proof casserole (like Corning Ware) or a metal baking pan with high sides.

3 oz. sliced pepperoni, chopped fine
3 1/2 c. all purpose flour
2 Tbsp. sugar
1 tsp. salt
1 tsp. freshly ground pepper
1 pkg. Rapid Rise yeast
2 Tbsp. unsalted butter, softened
1 1/4 c. hot water (125–130 degrees)

1. In the bowl of an electric mixer and using the paddle attachment, combine the pepperoni, flour, sugar, salt, pepper, yeast, and softened butter.
2. With the machine running, add the hot water in a steady stream. Beat until combined. The batter will be thick and sticky. Cover with a clean cloth and allow to rest 10 minutes.
3. Stir the dough down and turn it into the buttered casserole. Cover with plastic wrap and let rise in a warm place until doubled in size, about 50 minutes.
4. Bake for 40–45 minutes until nicely browned.
5. Remove from the pan and cool on a wire rack.

Sausage Bread

(Yield: 3 loaves)

The bread can be baked then frozen, kept well wrapped, up to 2 months. Remove from the freezer and bring to room temperature. Unwrap and warm the bread in a 350-degree oven for about 15–20 minutes.

Preheat oven to 375 degrees

- 1 box Hot Roll Mix
- 1 lb. good quality sweet Italian sausage (with no fennel) or good quality sausage meat
- 8 oz. mozzarella, grated
- 1/2 lb. Genoa salami, cut in 1/2-inch strips
- 1 c. Parmesan cheese, freshly grated
- 1 c. fresh Italian parsley, minced

Dough (Hot Roll Mix Preparation):

1. Combine the flour and yeast in a large bowl. Mix well.
2. In a small saucepan, add the butter to the hot water and heat gently until the butter just melts.
3. In a small bowl, beat the egg with a fork. Make a well in the center of the flour mixture. Add the egg. Stir to mix.
4. Add the water/butter to the mixture and beat with a wooden spoon until the dough pulls away from the sides of the bowl.
5. Knead, briefly, on a lightly floured board until smooth. Shape into a ball, cover with plastic wrap, and let rise 30 minutes.

Filling:

1. Remove the sausage meat from the casing. Sauté in a large skillet until the meat just loses its pink color. Drain off the fat.
2. Coarsely chop the meat in a food processor. Transfer to a bowl and let the mixture cool completely before adding the mozzarella, salami, Parmesan cheese, and parsley. Mix well.

Egg wash:

In a small bowl, beat 1 egg with 1 tablespoon cold water.

Assembly:

1. Punch the dough down and divide into 3 equal pieces. Remove 1 piece and cover the remainder.
2. Lightly butter or line 2 10x15-inch baking sheets with parchment paper.
3. On a lightly floured work surface, stretch the dough using a rolling pin, to a 10x14-inch rectangle. With the long side facing you, and leaving a 1/2-inch border on all sides, spread 1/3 of the prepared filling
4. Starting at the long end, roll up tightly, jelly-roll fashion.
5. Seal ends and place on the baking sheet, seam-side down. Cover with a clean cloth while making the remaining two loaves. Two loaves can fit in 1 pan, leaving 3 inches between loaves.
6. Let the covered loaves rise again for 30 minutes.
7. When ready to bake, brush the tops and sides with the egg wash.
8. Bake in the middle of the oven for 25 minutes or until golden.
9. Transfer to a wire rack and allow to cool. Cut on the diagonal and serve warm or at room temperature.

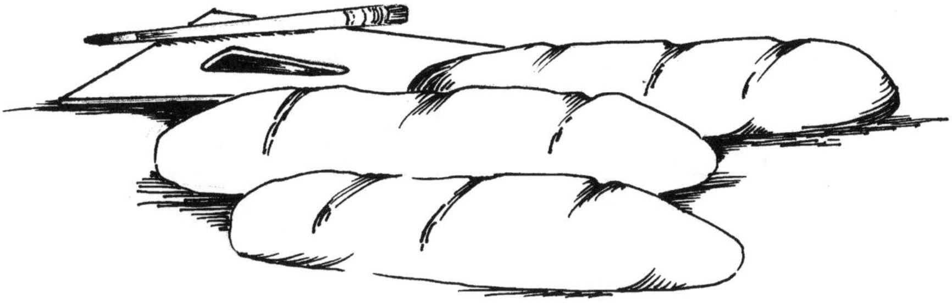

Focaccia with Sage
(A flat-bread with fresh sage leaves)

On Sunday morning in my father's bakery, when the night's work was done, the bakers created an early morning snack before heading home to sleep. Not a sweet treat, but a healthy light lunch made from the leftover bread dough, topped with olive oil, onions, and salt.

Focaccia can be many things: a warm appetizer dressed in herbs, tomatoes, olives, capers, and caramelized onions, or it can double as a delicious sandwich. The toppings and fillings are limitless: fresh sage and rosemary, prosciutto, pepperoni, onions, olive oil, grilled vegetables, tomatoes, mozzarella, sausage, and mushroom are just a few possibilities.

Try this recipe in a rectangular pan or in the cloche without the cover.

Preheat the oven to 400 degrees

1 pkg. active dry yeast
1 tsp. sugar
1 c. warm water, 105–115 degrees
3 Tbsp. olive oil
3 1/2 c. all purpose flour
10 fresh sage leaves, minced
1 tsp. salt
2 Tbsp. extra virgin olive oil
Sea salt to taste

1. In a small bowl, sprinkle the yeast and sugar in the water. Allow it to double in volume, about 10 minutes. Add 3 tablespoons olive oil.
2. In the bowl of an electric mixer, add the flour and salt.
3. Using the dough hook, gradually add the yeast mixture and beat until a soft dough is formed. Knead for about 5 minutes, adding a tablespoon more of flour if the dough is too soft.
4. Shape the dough into a ball. Place in an oiled bowl, turning it once to bring the oiled side up.
5. Cover with plastic wrap and allow it to rise until doubled in volume, about 1 hour.

The risen dough:

1. Remove the risen dough to a work surface. Knead the minced sage leaves into the dough. Place it in a 9x12-inch pan or the bottom of the cloche, sprinkled with cornmeal. Dimple it all over with your knuckles.
2. Drizzle with extra-virgin olive oil. Sprinkle with sea salt.
3. Bake the focaccia 25–30 minutes or until golden.
4. Remove and place on a rack. Serve warm or at room temperature.

Boned Chicken in Wine Sauce

(Serves: 6–8)

This is such an easy a recipe to prepare, but it doesn't rise to the lofty heights required to be a star in today's cooking stratosphere. But it's tried and true and a staple in my recipe file.

Bisquick is the key. Dredging the chicken pieces first in Bisquick, (which contains leavening agents) and then in beaten egg creates a batter-like mixture. The recipe can be made up to two days ahead, or baked and held in the freezer up to 2 months, then re-heated.

WINE SUGGESTION: Pinot Grigio

Preheat the oven to 375 degrees

4 boneless chicken breasts, cut in medallion-size pieces
3 Tbsp. unsalted butter
3 Tbsp. corn oil
Bisquick for dredging
2 eggs, beaten with a fork
salt and freshly ground pepper to taste
1/2 c. dry white wine or dry vermouth

1. In a large skillet, heat the corn oil and butter.
2. On a piece of wax paper or on a paper plate, dredge the chicken in Bisquick and then in the beaten egg.
3. Sauté the pieces until golden on all sides.
4. Place the chicken pieces in an oven-proof 9x11x2-inch baking dish. Drizzle with wine. Add salt and pepper to taste.
5. Cover with foil and bake for 20 minutes.
6. Remove the foil and bake an additional 5 minutes.

Veal Stew

(Serves 8)

Preheat the oven to 375 degrees

4 Tbsp. unsalted butter
4 Tbsp. corn or olive oil
3 lbs. shoulder of veal, cut into 1-inch cubes
about 1 c. flour for dredging, spread on a paper plate or wax paper
salt and freshly ground pepper to taste
2 Tbsp. unsalted butter
2 tsp. chopped garlic
1 c. finely chopped onions
1/2 tsp. freshly grated nutmeg
1 c. dry white wine or dry vermouth
1 c. chicken broth
1 bay leaf
3/4 tsp. dried thyme
16 baby carrots
16 pearl onions
1 c. heavy cream
1 Tbsp. fresh lemon juice

1. Spread the flour on a paper plate or wax paper.
2. Sprinkle all the pieces of meat with salt and pepper.
3. In a 12-inch skillet (Do not use a non-stick pan. The meat will not brown nicely.) melt 4 tablespoons of the butter with the oil, (oil keeps the butter from burning) over medium heat.
4. Dredge the veal pieces in flour, coating them on all sides and shaking off the excess. Dredge the pieces in flour only when you are ready to add them to the pan. Lightly brown the meat, braising in batches. Remove the meat to a platter.

5. In a large, oven-proof casserole, melt 2 tablespoons butter. Add the onions, nutmeg and garlic and sauté to soften, about 3 minutes. Transfer the meat to the casserole.
6. Add the wine or vermouth and burn off the alcohol over medium heat, about 3 minutes.
7. Add the chicken broth, bay leaf, and thyme. Stir, cover, and place in the oven. Check after 30 minutes. Add 1/4 cup chicken stock if needed. Stir and return to the oven and cook for an additional 30 minutes.
8. Meanwhile, add the carrots and onions to a saucepan, cover with water, and bring to a boil. Add salt to taste and simmer 5 minutes. Drain.
9. Add the vegetables to the casserole. Add the cream and lemon juice and simmer on top of the stove for 15 minutes, stirring occasionally, or until the meat is tender.

Asparagus with Parmesan Cheese

Choose asparagus that are firm and with tips that are tightly closed.

2 lbs. asparagus
salt and freshly ground pepper to taste
4 Tbsp. unsalted butter
1/2 c. Parmesan cheese

1. Hold the asparagus spear at the tip end. Using a vegetable peeler, scrape away the tough, fibrous part of the stalk. Trim to even lengths.
2. Refresh in cold water for 15 minutes.
3. Steam the asparagus. Cook to *al dente.*
4. Arrange the spears in a buttered, rectangular oven-proof pan. Season with salt and pepper.
5. Dot with butter and sprinkle with the cheese.
6. Preheat the broiler. Place the pan at least 6 inches from the heating element. Broil until the cheese is crusty and golden.

Zucchini Soufflé

(Serves 8)

This vegetable dish works well with veal, chicken, or pork. Preparing the recipe partially ahead of time is the big plus here. The wine selection is determined by the meat.

Preheat the oven to 375 degrees

1 medium onion, chopped fine
2 Tbsp. olive oil
2 Tbsp. unsalted butter
2 lbs. zucchini, sliced about 1/4-inch thick
salt and freshly ground pepper to taste
2/3 c. water
1 tsp. dried oregano
4 eggs, beaten
1/2 c. unflavored breadcrumbs
1/2 c. Parmesan cheese, freshly grated

1. Cut the zucchini into thin slices. Use a food processor, if you have one.
2. In a 12-inch sauté pan, add the zucchini slices and water and simmer, covered, for 20 minutes.
3. Meanwhile, add the chopped onion to a small fry pan containing the oil and butter. Sauté until limp.
4. When the zucchini are cooked, drain off the liquid and reserve.
5. Transfer the zucchini to a food processor and puree.
6. Transfer the puree, the reserved liquid, and the sautéed onion to a large bowl.
7. Add the salt, pepper, oregano, breadcrumbs, and cheese. *The recipe can be made and held at this point. Add the beaten eggs just before placing in the oven.*
8. Butter a 1 1/2-qt. oven-proof casserole.
9. Stir the beaten eggs into the zucchini mixture and spoon into the casserole.
10. Bake for about 50–60 minutes.

Sally Lunn—For the Morning After

(Yield: 1 large loaf or 2 small loaves)

Another no-knead bread, a delectable breakfast treat for the morning after a dinner party.

2 9x5-inch loaf pans or 1 large angel food pan, buttered
1/2 c. warm water (105–115 degrees)
1 pkg. active dry yeast
1 c. warm milk
1/4 lb. (1 stick) unsalted butter, softened
1/4 c. sugar
2 tsp. salt
3 large eggs, well beaten, at room temperature
5 1/2 to 6 c. unsifted all purpose flour

1. In a small saucepan, heat the milk until bubbles form on the edge of the pan. Remove from the heat.
2. Add the butter, sugar, and salt and stir until the butter is melted. Set aside to cool to room temperature.
3. Meanwhile, sprinkle the yeast over warm water in the large bowl of a standing mixer. Gently swirl the bowl to dissolve the yeast.
4. Using the paddle attachment, add the milk mixture, eggs, and some of the flour.
5. At medium speed, beat the mixture, adding flour a cupful at a time. Add enough flour to form a sticky batter.
6. Cover, let rise in a warm place, until doubled in bulk, about 1 1/2 hours.
7. Stir down and spoon into prepared pans.
8. Cover and let rise in a warm place until doubled in bulk, about 1 hour.
9. Bake the large loaf 30 minutes at 400 degrees or until a cake tester comes out clean. Bake the small loaves at 375 degrees for 30 minutes or until done.
10. Remove from the pans immediately and cool on wire racks. Sally Lunn freezes well.

Biscotti—A Dunking Cookie, Maybe

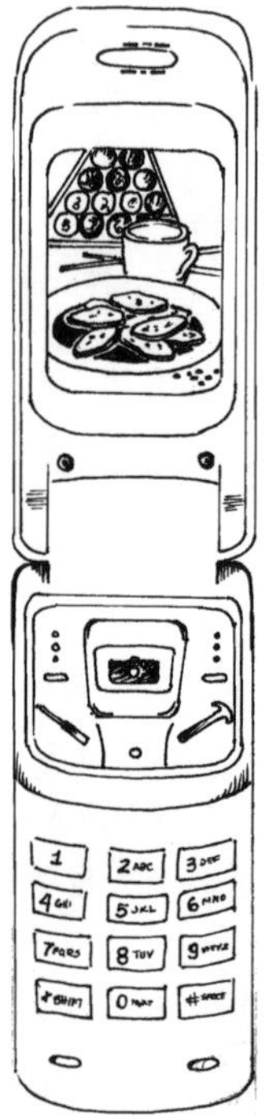

Biscotti have taken America by storm. These twice-baked cookies fill the bill as an impromptu dinner dessert, accompanied by a delicious cup of cappuccino. Biscotti, however, are not relegated to an after-dinner confection. Anise-flavored biscuits go hand in glove with a café latte for breakfast. Most biscotti are low in fat and sugar; a fact that appeals to health-conscious Americans.

The word *biscotti* has a dual meaning. In Italian, *Bis* means "more than one" and *cotto* means "cooking." The dough is shaped into logs and baked once. Then the logs are cut on the diagonal and returned to the oven to bake a second time. The word *biscotti* is also a generic term that denotes many different types of Italian cookies.

First and foremost on the biscotti banner is Biscotti di Prato, an ultra crisp, not-too-sweet cookie laden with almonds. They were created by Datini in the fourteenth century in Prato, a city near Florence, and were served with a glass of Vin Santo—a dry to sweet Tuscan wine similar to sherry. The biscotti list, however, doesn't stop there. Prolific Italian and American chefs have created biscotti made with butter, chocolate, and all varieties of nuts, dried fruits, and spices.

Baking Tips:

1. Use unsalted butter, not margarine.
2. If you are working with a soft mixture, spoon the dough onto the pan forming a rough log, and then even out the sides with floured hands or a pastry knife.
3. Line the pan with parchment paper for easy cleanup.
4. Use a serrated knife for slicing.
5. Allow logs to cool for 5 minutes before slicing on a cutting board.
6. Return the sliced cookies to the oven, laying them cut side down for a crispy cookie, or standing straight up to dry if it contains chocolate or fruit.
7. Cool the biscotti on a rack before storing in airtight containers.

Biscotti di Prato

(Yield: approximately 3 1/2 dozen)

3/4 c. whole almonds, toasted, cooled, and cut into rough halves

3 large eggs

1 tsp. vanilla

1/4 tsp. almond extract

2 c. flour

1 c. sugar

1 tsp. baking soda

pinch salt

1. Put the almonds on a baking sheet and bake at 350 degrees for 8–10 minutes. Cool. Using a cleaver or chef's knife, cut the nuts into rough halves. Set aside.
2. Reduce the oven temperature to 300 degrees.
3. Butter and flour a baking sheet or line with parchment paper.
4. In a small bowl, beat the eggs, vanilla, and almond extract with a whisk.
5. In the mixing bowl of an electric mixer, add the flour, sugar, baking soda, and salt.
6. Add the egg mixture to the dough and stir until blended, about 1 minute. Mix in the nuts. Do not overwork the dough.
7. Divide the dough in half. Spoon out the dough, forming 2 logs, 1/2-inch thick, 1 1/2-inches wide and 14 inches long and spaced about 2 inches apart. Even out the sides using floured hands.
8. Bake in a preheated 300-degree oven for 50 minutes or until golden brown. Cool the logs in the pan for 5 minutes.
9. Remove the logs to a cutting board and using a serrated knife, slice them 1/2-inch thick on the diagonal. Reduce the oven temperature to 275 degrees.
10. Lay the slices flat on the baking sheet and return to the oven for 20 to 25 minutes or until toasted, turning them over once to dry on the other side. Cool completely before storing.

Anise Biscotti

(Yield: Approximately 3 1/2 dozen)

2/3 c. whole almonds, toasted in a 350-degree oven for 8–10 minutes, then cooled.
1 Tbsp. Anise seeds
1/2 c. unsalted butter
3/4 c. sugar
2 large eggs
2 c. flour
1 1/2 tsp. baking powder
1/4 tsp. salt

1. In a mixing bowl, cream the butter and sugar together until light and fluffy.
2. Beat in the eggs.
3. On a paper plate or piece of wax paper, combine the flour, baking powder, salt, and anise seeds.
4. Add to the creamed mixture until just combined.
5. Using a cleaver or chef's knife, cut the nuts in half or thirds and fold into the mixture.
6. Divide the dough in half. On a greased and floured or parchment-lined baking sheet, form the dough into 2 logs about 1 1/2-inches wide and 14 inches long, spaced about 2 inches apart.
7. Bake at 325 degrees for 25 minutes or until lightly browned.
8. Cool 5 minutes and transfer to a board. Slice 1/2-inch thick on the diagonal.
9. Return to the oven for 10 minutes to dry slightly. Cool on racks and store in an airtight container.

Tiramisu: The Supreme "Pick-me-up"

(Serves 16)

Tiramisu is a kissin' cousin to Trifle, its English counterpart. But the history lesson stops there. The authentic origins of tiramisu are hazy to say the least. We do know, however, that tiramisu was created in Venice toward the end of the eighteenth century, and literally means, in the Venetian dialect, "pick me up."

There are many variations of this airy, mousse-like dessert. Whenever I'm in a quandary and can't decide what to serve at a special dinner party or family celebratory event, this tiramisu recipe beckons to me from my recipe file.

The essentials for success:

Mascarpone cheese: Italian double cream cheese, either domestic or imported, and available in most supermarkets and specialty shops.

Savoiardi: The Italian equivalent of Ladyfingers: a sponge-like biscuit, made of finger-shaped pieces of paste covered with sifted sugar and joined together in pairs; and usually imported from Italy. They are unlike the soft spongy ladyfingers that are sold in supermarkets or bakeries.

Espresso: Double strength espresso. Dip the Savoiardi on each side in the espresso for 1 to 2 seconds. Do not soak them.

The cake must be made a day in advance and refrigerated.

10x12-inch baking dish.
32 Savoiardi
2 c. Espresso coffee, cooled
6 large eggs, separated
1/2 c. sugar
1 lb. Mascarpone
4 oz. good quality semisweet chocolate, shaved or chopped fine
2 Tbsp. light rum

1. Make the espresso. Cool. Put the coffee into a flat bowl.
2. Separate the eggs. In the bowl of a standing mixer, and using the paddle attachment, beat the yolks with the sugar until light yellow in color.
3. Add the Mascarpone and beat at medium speed until combined.
4. Add the rum and combine. Transfer the mixture to a large bowl.

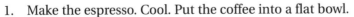

5. Thoroughly wash and dry the stand mixer bowl. Put the egg whites in the bowl, and using the wire whisk attachment, beat the whites until stiff but not dry.
6. Using a rubber spatula, gently fold about one-quarter of the whites into the Mascarpone mixture to lighten it. Fold in the remaining whites, taking care not to deflate them. The mixture will be soft.
7. Briefly dip each Savoiardi in the espresso, arranging 8 in two horizontal columns, 16 in all, snugly fit side by side, in a 10x12-inch pan.
8. Spread half the Mascarpone mixture on the ladyfingers. Sprinkle with half the chocolate gratings.
9. Repeat the procedure to make the second layer. Cover with foil or plastic wrap and refrigerate for 24 hours or overnight.
10. When ready to serve, cut the tiramisu into square portions with a metal spatula and serve on dessert plates.

The recipe is easily halved. Use a single row of biscuits, arranged in a 7x14-inch rectangular serving dish.

Move Over Tiramisu: Let Me Introduce You to Panna Cotta

Tiramisu's popularity is due in no small measure to its appearance in so many guises. The originality of these masquerades contributes to its lasting acclaim.

But along comes a rival for the affection of a dessert lover—the elegant Panna Cotta, or Cooked Cream. It's a simple, make-ahead dessert, and a boon to the busy cook.

Panna Cotta

(Yield: 6 servings)

1 pkg. unflavored gelatin
4 Tbsp. whole milk
2 1/4 c. heavy cream
1/2 c. confectioners' sugar
1/4 tsp. vanilla extract

Garnish:

Fresh raspberries

1. Butter 6 small custard cups or soufflé molds.
2. In a small bowl, soften the gelatin in the milk, for 10 minutes.
3. In a medium saucepan, combine the cream and sugar.
4. Bring the mixture to a boil to dissolve the sugar.
5. Remove from the heat. Blend in the softened gelatin and vanilla.
6. Pour the mixture into the prepared molds and chill 2 hours or until set.
7. To unmold: dip the molds in hot water for 30 seconds and invert onto individual dessert plates.
8. Garnish with fresh raspberries.

Biscuit Tortoni

(Serves 6)

Lazzaroni di Saronno cookies are imported from Italy. They come individually packed in various tissue colors in an attractive red tin. The cookies have a long shelf life.

1 c. crushed Amaretti cookies
1/4 c. sugar
pinch salt
3/4 c. whole milk
8 oz. heavy cream
1/2 tsp. vanilla extract
1/4 tsp. almond extract

1. Using a rolling pin, pulverize the Amaretti cookies on a piece of wax paper. Reserve 1/4 cup.
2. Transfer 3/4 cup cookie crumbs to a medium bowl.
3. Stir in the sugar and salt.
4. Stir in the milk.
5. Allow the mixture to stand for 15 minutes.
6. Whip the cream and add the extracts.
7. Carefully fold the flavored cream into the cookie crumb mixture.
8. Spoon into ramekins or soufflé dishes.
9. Sprinkle the tops with the reserved crumbs.
10. Cover with plastic wrap or foil and freeze until firm.
11. When ready to serve, remove from the freezer 15 minutes before serving.

Wine Terminology

Acetic	Sharp taste of vinegar
Balance	Harmony of the fruit, tannin, and acid
Body	The feel of substance in the mouth
Bouquet	Fragrance
Character	Distinctive taste characteristics
Clean	A well made wine with no *off* taste
Delicate	Light, young, and fresh
Dry	Not sweet or sour
Elegant	Well balanced
Flinty	Dry, clean, sharp
Fresh	Young, lively, and clean
Full	Rich in fruit flavors
Light	Lacking in body but pleasant
Mellow	Mature, soft
Noble	Superior, impressive
Nose	Aroma and bouquet
Oxidized	Off taste from contact with the air
Robust	Big and full wine
Round	Well balanced, mature
Sharp	Acidy
Soft	Mellow
Sour	Vinegar, not fit to drink
Spritzy	Slightly sparkling usually in young wines
Sweet	High sugar content
Tart	Acidity high
Thin	No body, watery
Velvety	Soft, silky texture
Woody	Undesirable odor of wood
Yeasty	Pleasant taste in many types of champagnes

The Partnership of Wine and Cheese

Careful thought should be given to the pairing of cheese and wine. Some cheeses may be too strong for lighter wines and conversely, some mild cheeses cannot stand up to bold, full-bodied wines. The combination of wine and cheese fills the bill for a light lunch or a picnic, but the best time to enjoy cheese and wine is as an integral part of the meal, just after the main course or as a dessert.

Bel Paese, mild and creamy	Sauvignon Blanc, Dry Riesling
Brie	Beaujolais, Zinfandel, Chianti
Camembert	Cabernet Sauvignon, Bordeaux
Cheddar	Full-bodied reds or whites
Mild Cheddar	Light-bodied wines
Edam	Chablis, Sauvignon Blanc, Beaujolais
Fontina	Bardolino, Valpolicella
Gorgonzola	Amarone, Barolo, Port
Gruyere	Chardonnay, Cabernet Sauvignons
Jarlsberg	Sauvignon Blanc
Monterey Jack	Dry Whites
Mozzarella	Verdicchio, Chenin Blanc
Parmesan (sliced)	Chianti, Cabernet, Zinfandel
Port Salut	Chianti, Young Zinfandels
Provolone	Barolo, Petit Sirah, Zinfandel
Roquefort	Barolo, Port
Stilton	Burgundy, Port

The Partnership of Wine and Food

The perfect wine makes any meal a memorable one. Two factors to consider in the selection process are how the food is seasoned and not necessarily whether it's fish, fowl, or meat. Is the food spicy or is it smoky? The following pairings are merely guidelines. The bottom line, drink the wine that you like.

Caviar	Champagne
Shellfish	Fumé Blanc, Chablis, Pinot Blanc
Grilled Salmon	Pinot Noir
Poached Salmon	Chardonnay
Freshwater Fish	Chenin Blanc, Fumé Blanc
Grilled Chicken	Fumé Blanc
Roast Chicken	Cabernet Sauvignon
Creamed Chicken	Chardonnay
Beef as steak or roast	Cabernet Sauvignon
Beef with a tomato sauce	Zinfandel
Veal	Chardonnay
Lamb as chops	Zinfandel
Roast Lamb	Cabernet Sauvignon
Roast Pork	Gamay Beaujolais
Pork as chops	Zinfandel
Ham	White Zinfandel, Grenache Rosé

Glossary of Culinary Terms and Definitions

Al dente:	Italian phrase to describe pasta cooked only until it offers a slight resistance when bitten into, not soft or overdone.
Balsamella:	Italian for Béchamel
Balsamic vinegar:	Made from white Trebbiano grapes, aged in barrels of various sizes and woods for at least ten years in the area surrounding Modena.
Blanch:	Plunge vegetables or fruit into boiling water briefly, then into cold water to stop the cooking process.
Blend:	Combine ingredients by hand, with a whisk, blender, or electric mixer until the ingredients are completely incorporated.
Cook onions until softened:	Cooking onions until they have lost their moisture content and become translucent.
Deglaze:	Heat small amounts of liquid in the pan after the fat has been removed, stirring to loosen brown bits of food adhering to the pan. Water, wine, or stock is used.
Dice:	Cut ingredients into small even cubes.
Fold:	A technique used to gently combine a light, airy mixture with a heavier mixture. The lighter mixture is placed on top of the heavier one in a large bowl. Starting at the back of the bowl, a rubber spatula is used to cut down vertically through the two mixtures. The bowl is rotated a quarter turn with each series of strokes.
Poach:	Cook poultry, fish, or meat in gently simmering water or stock.

Pancetta:	Italian bacon cured with salt and spices but not smoked. It is formed into a sausage-like roll.
Prosciutto:	Cured ham, unsmoked and uncooked: The finest prosciutto comes from Parma, Friuli, and Veneto.
Purée:	Reduce a solid to a smooth, creamy consistency using a blender, food processor, or sieve.
Ragu:	A hearty meat and tomato sauce for pasta.
Sauté:	Cook food quickly in a skillet in a small amount of oil or butter or both until browned.
Simmer:	Cook food gently in a liquid at a low temperature.
Soffrito:	Chopped aromatic herbs and vegetables lightly fried in butter and oil.

About the Author

PATRICIA GAMBARELLI is an accomplished culinary writer and teacher. Though she started out in the field of chemistry, Patricia switched career paths to satisfy a desire to teach as well as to indulge her passion for her Italian heritage. She taught cooking classes for eleven years (including the *Pasta for Men Only* classes that inspired this book), and has served as Food and Wine Editor for Long Island and North Carolina newspapers. Patricia served on the Board of Directors for the New York Association of Cooking Teachers, was a member of the International Association of Culinary Professionals, and has studied under master chefs, including Guliano Bugialli and Marcella Hazan. She has also served as Culinary Director for the Long Island Wine and Food Society, and participated in several projects for the James Beard Foundation. After moving to North Carolina, she organized and now directs the Sea Trail Gourmet Group, serving upwards of 100 participants. *Pasta for Men Only* is her first book.

About the Artist

SUZANNE HUNADY has taught art at the elementary, junior high, and high school levels. She has also taught specialized courses in art centers and colleges and has extensive experience in teaching exceptional children. Sue has been highly recognized for her work in teaching and has been cited both in Ohio and North Carolina as the outstanding teacher of the year. She most recently won the TIEFF-Cref Leaders in Learning and Liberty Outstanding Teacher Award. While Sue works in several mediums, she specializes in watercolors and acrylics. She has exhibited and won awards for her work in Ohio, Michigan, and North Carolina.